WITHDRAWN

D0534102

Mana... ...ilitie

This book is dedicated to our respective husbands, children and mothers, without whom we would have been unable to achieve our goal.

Christine Jones
Valerie Jowett

Managing facilities

Christine Jones
and
Valerie Jowett

This book is dedicated to our respective husbands, children and mothers, without whom we would have been unable to achieve our goal   Christine Jones and Valerie Jowett

Butterworth-Heinemann
Linacre House, Jordan Hill, Oxford OX2 8DP
225 Wildwood Avenue, Woburn MA 01801-2041
A division of Reed Educational and Professional Publishing Ltd

A member of the Reed Elsevier plc group

OXFORD   AUCKLAND   BOSTON
JOHANNESBURG   MELBOURNE   NEW DELHI

First published 1998
Transferred to digital printing 2001

British Library Cataloguing in Publication Data
A catalogue record for this book is available from the British Library

ISBN 0 7506 3135 X

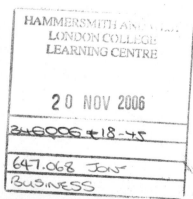

346006

Contents

Preface

This book has been written primarily for hotel, hospitality and facilities managers. Practising managers and students of hospitality management and facilities management will find it of value.

The book gives concise, up-to-date information, applying generic management concepts in a practical way to facilities management. The aim is to put facilities management into the context of hotels, showing the benefits of a facilities management approach to this area. Plenty of practical examples are given throughout.

The purpose of the book is to provide an analysis of facilities management and apply the concepts in a practical way in the context of hospitality management, with emphasis on hotels.

Included in the book is a definition of facilities management and an analysis of the development of this concept. The benefits of a facilities management approach are discussed and the significance of a strategic approach to facilities. An analysis of hotels' physical assets, in the context of the core product or 'service package' sold to guests is provided. Contracting out and outsourcing are identified as important considerations in facilities management and the process of procuring services is discussed, together with the development of service level agreements.

Approaches to managing and monitoring of service operations are developed. The book also looks at the benefits to be derived from investing in people (staff and customers) and summarizes by looking at processes which enable the hotel to develop a competitive edge, including quality improvement, productivity and yield management.

1
The concept and scope of facilities management

Aims and objectives

This chapter aims to:

- identify the scope and meaning of facilities management
- identify the value of facilities management in hotels
- consider why facilities management has developed
- identify trends in the continuing development of facilities management.

What is facilities management?

There are many definitions and interpretations of the term 'facilities management'. The British Institute for Facilities Management (1996) defines it as:

> *The practice of co-ordinating the physical workspace with the people and work of an organisation, (it) integrates the principles of business administration, architecture and the behavioural and engineering sciences.*

As the overview of this definition (Figure 1.1) shows, facilities management represents broad ranging issues.

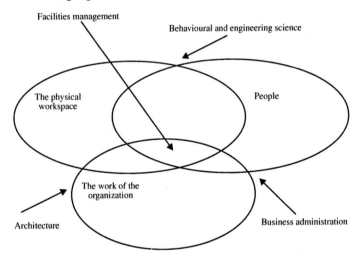

Figure 1.1 The overview of facilities management.

What value does facilities management have to hotels?

If facilities management is about managing physical assets, it has considerable relevance to hotels and other hospitality businesses, as the property or the premises in which the hospitality is delivered, form a major part of the product package sold to customers.

Customer needs could be for overnight accommodation, a meeting area or a restaurant meal. In each case, the physical assets will form an important part of the product. Some of the common elements required to produce the 'accommodation product' are shown in Figure 1.2.

Guests might also require:

● a source of information (e.g. regarding the other amenities)
● privacy
● secretarial assistance

- porterage
- car-parking space
- ramp access
- lifts
- personal laundry service
- sleeping facilities.

As can be seen, the physical assets are prominent. The list could go on. Whereas many of the identified needs of customers are tangible (e.g. the lift, the guestroom and the hot water) and relate to physical assets, other needs (e.g. security and feeling of well-being) are largely intangible.

Since the accommodation forms a major part of the product, even in small hotels, the capital outlay or revenue expenditure on the property is proportionately high compared with other businesses. In order for business to be conducted in an hotel, it is *essential* for at least certain of the physical assets to be actively managed. Although the term 'facilities management' might not be used, elements of facilities management would need to be applied to hotels to achieve business success.

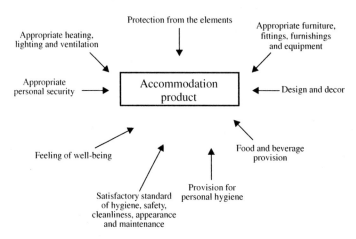

Figure 1.2 The 'accommodation' product.

The development of facilities management

A property-based discipline

Facilities management as a practice has its roots in the USA, where development took place during the 1980s. It is evolving from a property-based discipline concerned with *reactive, operational* aspects of property management, services and maintenance (including cleaning, 'caretaking', waste disposal and catering) into a much more *proactive, strategic* role. In this role, it is also concerned with the design of property and the work environment, purchasing, and future management and maintenance of the property – thus, it covers a broad area of 'non-core' activities (see Figure 1.3). Such activities could include IT services and even human resources management. It

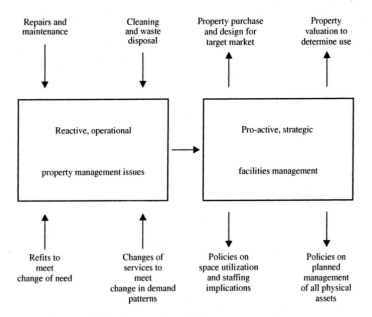

Figure 1.3 The evolution of facilities management.

is this strategic role of facilities management which will be developed in this book.

From a management perspective, facilities management must consider the needs of all building users, together with the needs of others who may be affected by the management of the building. The needs of the following people, therefore, have to be considered.

- **Shareholders** have an interest in business and property values and the asset value and service standards must be maintained or developed.
- **Employees** need an efficient working environment. This is conducive to high morale and to high quality and productivity.
- **Customers** in an hotel will not only be visiting the establishment, they will, hopefully, enjoy using its facilities. Considerable expertise must go into creating an atmosphere and environment which reinforces the good image of the organization.
- **The local community** will be affected by the property. Aspects such as visual appearance, pollution, traffic (as a result of business), employment and the encouragement of local custom must all be managed.
- **Reliable suppliers** who provide consistent quality are very important to the success of any organization. They might be providing a service, staff, equipment or supplies. Partnerships, strategic alliances and other agreements are some means by which this group can be managed.

Figure 1.4 summarizes the scope of facilities management to meet the needs of these different stakeholders.

Recent history gives some indication as to how and why the concept of facilities management, in general, not just in the hospitality industry, has developed in the last decade and suggests that although many of the strands are not new, the overall approach does have a different emphasis.

The various factors which may have attributed to the rise in facilities management will now be considered.

Figure 1.4 The scope of facilities management.

Factors attributing to the development of facilities management

Cost reductions

Fierce competition, depressed trading conditions, higher energy costs and other economic elements have forced companies to look at all means of reducing costs and maintaining the market edge. Facilities costs can be very significant. Stipanuk and Roffman (1992) estimated that a full service hotel of under 125 rooms has an average expense of 11.9 per cent of turnover for property management and energy. With respect to on-going energy and maintenance costs, savings can best be made at the design stage of buildings. The development of ideas on terotechnology (considering life-cycle costs at the planning stage) is yet another probable stimulus for the development of facilities management concepts.

In response to the rising awareness of property costs, attempts have been made to forecast total ownership costs of buildings (life-cycle costs) at the planning stage. These costs would include:

Initial (fixed costs) + Operating costs + Residual costs
(e.g. demolition or sale).

Initial costs

These represent the largest single cost (often more than 30 per cent of the total asset value), but account for less than 50 per cent of the total ownership cost of an organization. The proportion of costs relating to the initial outlay will, of course, vary with the use of the building. The Forte Group was considered to be the fourth largest 'property company' in the UK in terms of value of assets held, prior to its acquisition in 1995. More recently, the popularity of system building has increased. By this process, to varying degrees, hotels can be prefabricated in a factory and assembled on site. This reduces not only the time to be allowed for construction (this can be less than 20 weeks) but reduces initial costs.

Operating costs

If these are available at the premises purchasing stage, they provide an excellent planning tool. However, operating costs are difficult to predict (Lee, 1987). The main reasons being as follows.

- Lack of appropriate data on which to base forecasts – if the expected life of a building is taken to be 40 years, even where detailed operating costs have been recorded in a property (which is uncommon, particularly where ownership has changed), it is improbable that a similar building will be planned. It is more likely that technological developments and different user needs will mean that modifications are made and, thus, the recorded data has reduced value as a planning tool.
- Changes in technology, which could relate to the development of new materials with different characteristics from those currently used. There could also be development of new maintenance materials or equipment, different methods and different outcomes of maintenance.
- Historical data does not represent current needs, in other words, if the budget of an organization at any moment in the life span of a building is very limited, then only essential maintenance will be carried out.
- Since there are so many probabilities involved, the level of prediction involved is too great.

A standard method of collecting building operating cost data was devised by Building Maintenance Information Limited (BMI). They gave a definition of the items to be included in 'operation costs' as:

- cleaning (internal and external)
- maintenance
- utilities
- administrative (i.e. salaries, wages and insurance of service attendants, laundry, porterage, security, rubbish disposal, property management and overheads such as property insurance and rates).

Research by Hajj (1991) into buildings' operating costs shows the total annual running costs of all categories of building as:

- 16 per cent maintenance
- 18 per cent cleaning
- 20 per cent utilities
- 21 per cent administration
- 25 per cent overheads.

However, the reliability of these predictions is difficult to assess, bearing in mind the 40-year life of a building.

Residual costs

These relate to disposal cost, which might involve selling on or demolition. Again, this is a very difficult aspect to estimate.

The high cost of space, by lease, construction or upgrading is forcing detailed analysis of true space needs and space costs within organizations and the management of space has become an area of specialism.

Competition has compelled businesses to develop policies for the efficient use of space, equipment and furniture. In addition, a coordinated approach is needed. Property strategies need to be formulated in conjunction with organizational strategies. A depressed economy forces focus on improving operational efficiency.

Change in organizational structures

A developing characteristic of organizational structures, noted in the UK and the USA, is the tendency towards flatter structures with fewer tiers. Organizational restructuring and the shedding of middle management is driven in part by the need for greater efficiency and, perhaps, by more effective IT in core business activities. One result of this has been the development and extension of sub-contracting to areas such as facilities management, a trend certainly seen in hotels. Downsizing (or 'rightsizing') has increased the use of management consultancies, including facilities management.

Legislation and Government policies

In the UK, compulsory, competitive tendering 'market testing', as Government policy, has been enforced within public centre organizations. In 1980, the term 'privatization' was first applied when the Ministry of Defence contracted out most of its building cleaning. This represented the prospect of £20 million of new work for contractors. In 1983, the Government required health authorities to invite competitive tenders and, in 1988, the Local Government Act made competitive tendering by local authorities compulsory.

Over the years, compulsory competitive tendering has been a controversial issue, but certainly growth of specialist contract companies has been stimulated. More recently, contract companies offering management expertise in a wide range of activities have developed. Advantages have been seen in the 'one cheque' approach (i.e. paying one company to manage a range of services), which is often referred to as 'total' or 'integrated' facilities management.

This has encouraged organizations to focus on their core activities and to buy in other services. Hence, the stimulus for the growth in servicing or 'facilities management' companies.

Health and safety legislation since the Health and Safety at Work Act (1974) has also been considerable and has necessitated a planned and systematic approach, led by senior management. Expertise has often been bought in from specialist companies and a similar route is likely to be taken following legislation relating to waste management and energy management.

The need for flexibility

Continuous change of policy, market and methods within organizations is now common. Whereas once, such decisions and changes were momentous and seen to be long-lasting, now they are considered to be more routine. At one time, there was only an occasional need for someone to oversee change, whereas now that person is needed full-time. Changes related to physical assets include extending or reducing overall working space, modifying workstations to facilitate changing work methods or achieving building modifications in line with 'rate of churn' (i.e. movement of personnel within jobs in the building). Obsolescence related to workspace rarely means physical decay, it often means the right fabric in the wrong place. Such a process of change has been evidenced in hotels with relation to computerization and in restaurants as eating habits change and customer expectations of environment alter.

In addition, response time needs to be fast. Downtime is waste. Hotel rooms are a perishable commodity as those not sold tonight cannot be sold twice tomorrow night. Acknowledgement of the facilities as a major resource of the business itself, often means that premises are used round the clock. Guest rooms in hotels are used as seminar or meeting rooms during the day. Heavier use demands more management.

Due to the more dynamic nature of organizations – involving moving premises, renting or sub-letting – an expertise has developed within the organizations. Whereas, in the past, a number of outside specialists might be required to provide the necessary advice and expertise, the experienced facilities manager with inside knowledge of the organization, can be better placed than the outside professionals to provide accurate briefs which address the specific requirements of that organization.

Further, industry in general has felt the impact of the increased use of teleworking (although with respect to hotels, effects will be limited to only the large ones). One of the effects of teleworking and, as a result, flexible working has been the changing demand for more flexible premises (particularly those related to office functions). In the past, office space in businesses was allocated on a permanent basis to each member of staff. Now, this is not always needed. Office space might only be needed occasionally by any one individual and the cost of holding under-utilized space has been highlighted. To optimize on the use of space, it can be allocated only when needed. Therefore, accommodation is shared and must be effectively scheduled and managed. Alternatively, some establishments have dispensed with much of their office accommodation and simply rent space as and when they need it. Some hotels have identified this concept as a business opportunity, letting rooms, on a 9 am to 5 pm basis to be used by such businesses for office accommodation.

Information Technology

Advances in IT for communications within the business context (e.g. for 'intelligent buildings'; and operating security, heating, lighting, ventilation controls and advance lifts) have demanded specialist skills.

Not only has the degree of usage of computers increased, in addition there is an increasing number of applications to which computers can be put. IT is not an 'add on' feature – it needs detailed consideration at the design stage of any new building or refurbishment. It must be an integral and flexible part of the facility.

IT may well be used to maintain the environmental conditions required, to assist in space management and in many other facility management functions. Specialist skills are needed for the management of such systems, an 'odd jobs person' will not suffice.

Obviously, IT used for telecommunications, teleconferencing, video conferencing and many other business functions also calls for specialist help and many organizations have been quick to identify this specialism as appropriate for outsourcing.

Employee needs and expectations

Although building operating costs are significant and demand careful management, such costs are relatively small when compared to staffing costs. This is particularly true in the hospitality industry and other service industries which are labour intensive.

Nevertheless, decisions involving expenditure in a small cost centre (e.g. property operating costs) can be used favourably to influence those in a large cost centre (e.g. labour). A little spent on facilities can provide disproportionate benefits for the people who work in the organization.

Good working conditions may influence recruitment (particularly of the young, which is important when demographic trends are considered), staff morale and productivity. Expectations regarding the working environment are rising with the increasing numbers of white-collared workers.

Identification of conditions such as sick building syndrome and repetitive strain injury raise the awareness of the possible undesirable effects of technology in the workplace and, in general, have heightened interest in working conditions. Certainly, claims against companies can be considerable if health and safety legislation is breached.

Linked with health and safety issues are those related to security. Risk assessments show that security of staff and customers (as well as property) is becoming a major consideration and security systems are becoming ever more sophisticated. Swipe cards to operate guest room's locks are now quite common and, again, these are supported by computers, creating yet another demand for specialist knowledge.

On security issues, another incentive for owners or managers to implement high security systems is the lower insurance cover demanded and the reduction in claims.

Management and customer perceptions

Finally, something which has always been evident in hotels, but less so in some other industries, is that facilities are not just seen as a capital asset to be bought and sold for their exchange value, but as a business asset, which can provide value simply through effective performance. Facilities management has the role of transforming an organization's building or stock of buildings from an overhead into a company resource.

Attractive, well-run facilities help the prestige and reputation of the organization in the eyes of customers and the community. In the hospitality industry this is particularly important. In hotels the property forms part of the product package sold to customers. A good visual impact is required in order to attract customers in the first place and their perception of the hotel experience will certainly be affected by appearance. The fact that customer expectations do not remain static, but are constantly changing, must also be addressed.

It can be seen, therefore, that facilities management has developed, partly through demand-led elements (e.g. the need for cost reductions, flexibility and specialism) and partly through increased supply (e.g. stimulated by competitive tendering and technological advances by specialists). These influences are summarized in Figure 1.5.

Trends in the development of facilities management

Many changes in recent years have been technological (e.g. building design and telecommunications). At the same time, human needs and expectations have changed and there is a need to bridge the gap between the technical and human (see Figure 1.6).

In looking at the growth of facilities management in the UK, a number of trends become evident.

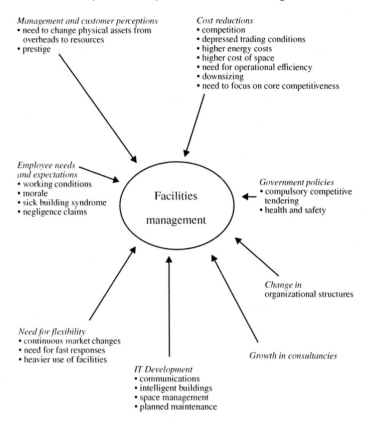

Management and customer perceptions
• need to change physical assets from overheads to resources
• prestige

Cost reductions
• competition
• depressed trading conditions
• higher energy costs
• higher cost of space
• need for operational efficiency
• downsizing
• need to focus on core competitiveness

Employee needs and expectations
• working conditions
• morale
• sick building syndrome
• negligence claims

Facilities management

Government policies
• compulsory competitive tendering
• health and safety

Change in organizational structures

Need for flexibility
• continuous market changes
• need for fast responses
• heavier use of facilities

IT Development
• communications
• intelligent buildings
• space management
• planned maintenance

Growth in consultancies

Figure 1.5 Recent pressures influencing the development of facilities management.

Increasing supply

There has been a rapid increase in the number of contractors offering services which fall under the scope of facilities management. The initial growth was for companies specializing in blue-collar, low-value work (e.g. catering and maintenance work). This area of work was not strategically sensitive.

Figure 1.6 The facilities management bridge.

The growth of contractors offering computing services led the way for the contracting out of more highly skilled functions, central to business success. 'White-collar', strategically sensitive work (e.g. 'front line staff') is now increasingly provided for by specialist contractors. This includes, in some cases, accounting functions and human resources management.

Single contract companies

As more work is contracted out, problems of dealing with so many contractors have become apparent. A demand has emerged for single contract companies to manage a range of services, providing a 'one cheque' approach.

In 1992, the Contract Cleaning and Maintenance Association changed its name to the Cleaning and Support Services Association, reflecting the emergence of this new market. Service companies often started in specialist, property-related fields (e.g. pest control, cleaning or catering), but have now extended their services. Services offered by one company may now include aspects of IT, personnel management, legal and accounting services, marketing, sales and distribution.

Partnerships

Partnerships and strategic alliances are developing between clients and contract companies in some areas. The facility manager can benefit from economies of scale, such as with integrated support services where the client has only one point of contact. In a partnership, improvements, cost reductions or other benefits developed by one party will have benefits for the other and both will share the rewards.

Vertical diversification

Whereas, in the past, construction companies handed buildings over to clients on their completion and ceased to be involved in the on-going life of that property, there is evidence that some construction companies are now becoming interested in the management of that building's life. Tarmac, for example, have developed their own facilities management offshoot and as buildings are built and sold or leased, many functions associated with the on-going development and maintenance of building functions are managed by their facilities management offshoot.

Benchmarking

In order to allow one organization to compare itself with others, with respect to space utilization efficiency, different benchmarking devices have been used. An office efficiency index was developed to benchmark the relative efficiency of businesses with respect to office space utilization. Various educational funding bodies consider the efficiency of space utilization as a measure in their funding rationale. Thus, facilities performance indicators or benchmarks are developed. It seems, however, that few business accounting systems disaggregate financial information in a form which assists the facilities manager and the standard system of hotel accounting is no exception.

Another difficulty relating to measuring efficiency is that customers and staff remain the most important asset. Facilities affect peoples' concentration, communication, access to resources, comfort, satisfaction, health and stress level. Reducing the fixed costs of assets and costs of certain provisions are measurable goals, measuring the effect of surroundings on staff or customers, is more difficult. Figure 1.7 summarizes these recent developments in the 'business' of facilities management.

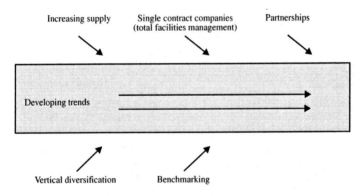

Figure 1.7 Developing trends in facilities management.

The value of facilities management for hotels

The hospitality industry has sometimes been accused of being introvert with respect to its application of management techniques and there is seen to be a need for generic management techniques to be applied to the field of hospitality.

Currently, facilities management is not a term generally applied within the hospitality industry. However, if the concept has roots within the field of property-based disciplines, there must be benefits of applying the concept within hotels – property being a major component of the product package.

In the 1990s, there have been spectacular commercial losses by shareholders in some hotel chains. The Queen's Moat House is one example. The losses were mainly attributed to changing-property values, one of the several aspects addressed by facilities management. Perhaps a facilities management approach could have value in preventing this sort of business failure.

Similarly, the take-over of the Forte Group by Granada highlighted the vast resources held by hotels with respect to physical assets. Surely a discipline which recognizes the strategic aspects of facilities offers potential for application within an hotel company.

In considering even small hotels (which represent the greatest proportion of all hotels), the capital outlay or revenue expenditure on the property is always going to be proportionately high when compared with many other small businesses, since the accommodation itself forms a major part of the product package offered to the customer. A strategic management process which optimizes the use of the property, therefore, must be worth investigation.

Although facilities management encompasses a range of activities which are not in themselves new (e.g. property maintenance), the concept advocates a more structured, integrated, strategic and holistic approach than is frequently applied. It is probable that many hotels are, in fact, operating elements of facilities management, but that they are not using this generic term.

Whose job is facilities management in an hotel?

As a strategic function, the responsibility for facilities management must lie with a senior manager but that manager might have different titles. In a small hotel, it would be the general manager his or herself. In a slightly larger hotel, facilities management might be the remit of the deputy manager. An alternative might be for the front of house manager to have responsibilities in this area or, indeed, for the responsibilities to be split between, for example, the executive housekeeper and the premises manager. In some of the chain hotels, the role of general manager has been replaced by regional management and, without doubt, there is a role for a manager at local level who has a facilities management remit.

The responsibility for facilities management must belong to an executive manager(s). The process will require that the manager translates organizational objectives, in the context of the overall mission, into plans for the development and maintenance of physical assets and services. There will need to be a deliberate coordination of people (i.e. staff, contractors, visitors and customers) and property.

The significant elements of facilities management

Facilities management may be interpreted differently in different hotels. The role of the facilities manager will vary according to the size of the hotel, the layers in the hierarchy, the degree to which work is outsourced and the overall objectives of the organization. However, the model in Figure 1.8 summarizes the significant elements of facilities management.

*See Chapter 2

Figure 1.8 A model to show the significant elements of facilities management.

As with modern management techniques such as continuous improvement programmes and the Investors in People initiative, facilities management first requires the identification of business objectives. It then follows a systematic process of management of the physical assets and other resources of an organization to achieve organizational effectiveness. The aim is to look holistically at the work environment – at its physical, cultural and organizational aspects.

References and further reading

Alexander, K. (1996) *Facilities Management Theory and Practice*. E. and F.N. Spon.

Barrett, P. (1992) *Facilities Management Research Directions*. University of Salford.

Burnham, J.M. (1994) *Integrative Facilities Management*. Irwin Professional Publishing.

Hajj, A.N.A. (1991) *Simple Cost-Significant Modes for Total Life Cycle Costing in Buildings*. PhD Thesis, University of Dundee.

Lee, R. (1987) *Building Maintenance Management*. Crosby, Lockwood and Staples.

Stipanuk, D. and Roffman, H. (1992) *Hospitality Facilities Management and Design*. The Educational Institute of The American Hotel and Motel Association.

2
The strategic planning role

Aims and objectives

This chapter aims to:

- identify the role of the mission statement and the strategic planning process in successful facilities management
- analyse the nature of service industries and the elements of the 'service package' offered to hotel guests
- consider the market, its segmentation and the elements of effective customer care
- evaluate the role and management of the customer in a customer-focused organization.

The changing working environment

Facilities management is evolving, not as an operational discipline reacting to immediate needs (e.g. making sure that rooms are cleaned), but in a strategic role, which encompasses forecasting and planning and which is capable of predicting and adapting to the changing needs of an organization. The objective of a strategic approach is that instead of an hotel being a victim of change, it is in fact master of that change.

Facilities management, whether in the context of hotels or in any other organization is operating in a fast changing world, in which changes need constantly to be monitored. Rather than reacting to change, however, the objective should be to predict and plan for it. Table 2.1 categorizes change factors into political, economic, social and technological influences and identifies current trends and some responses that have been made.

Table 2.1 A summary of changes and their likely impact on organizations

Category of change	Responses to and impact of change
Political pressures	
Changes in:	Employment legislation
● taxation	Availability of employment
● more laws	Health and safety, employment,
● political leadership	environmental legislation
● environmental policies	Outsourcing
Economic pressures	
Fluctuations in	Growth or death of companies,
● unemployment	mergers, take-overs
● inflation rates	Cut backs, 'down' or 'right' sizing
● interest rates	Achievement of efficiency gains
Globalization	No more 'jobs for life', need for
	life skills
	Portfolio careers
	Need to offer attractive
Increased competition for skilled	recruitment packages
staff	Uncertainty and change culture
	Loss of old markets, growth of
	new
	Constant scrutiny of productivity
	and performance
	Need for competitiveness
	Flexibility of service package
Market demand for products and	Customer focus
services	Definition of core business
Pricing policies	Project management
Delivery mechanisms	
Social pressures	
People expect and demand	Need for good working conditions
better quality of life	and flexible work patterns
Expect higher standards of service,	Increased incidence of litigation
hygiene, physical welfare,	Continuous improvement of hotel
education, healthcare, leisure	facilities

continued

Table 2.1 Continued

Category of change	Responses to and impact of change
Declining inclination to accept authority	Increase personal and team autonomy, delegation and empowerment Flatter structures
Declining loyalty	Increase financial and non-financial benefits and perks Need for increased job satisfaction and variety
Longer life expectancy and expect to be active for longer	Lifelong learning More older guests
Women taking fuller role in the workplace	Recruit and retain more women Provide childcare facilities
Increased awareness of environmental decline	Changes to working practices and chemicals used Use of natural resources in furniture and construction controlled
Pollution of land, water and air Lack of water	Recycling of heat and waste and reduction in amount Suppliers selected with discretion Plumbing fittings which conserve water
Technological pressures Computers, faxes, mobile phones, e-mail are commonplace Video and tele-conferencing developments Increased use of scanners, CD-Roms	Almost instantaneous communication Comprehensive employee, supplier and customer histories Decreased problem of geographical location Need for increased flexibility and fast response times Readily accessible data, information overload
Variety and availability of software Impact of world-wide web	Paperless offices Change in secretarial and administrative roles Greater access to wider customer bases Growth of computer training Impact on decision making
Electrical equipment cheaper	Increased automation

In the light of the need to be sensitive to changes in all categories, long-term planning of the facility must include consideration of its capacity, use of buildings and the resources needed to cope with changing demands, now and in the future. These must be planned with an awareness of changes and trends in the locality, nationally and internationally. Factors effecting the labour market, for example, will have a considerable affect on a labour-intensive industry such as hotels.

Facilities management, therefore, is driven by factors such as life-cycle costs, productivity, performance values and legislative change. Facilities management is about organizational effectiveness and competencies and planning, not just operations. The planning function relates to maximizing the use of a company's assets.

Although a number of the services which comprise facilities management can be contracted out, the strategic decisions that ensure that the business needs are being met and the accountability for the service will remain in-house. The facilities manager must have both strategic responsibility and remit.

What is strategic management?

Strategic management involves looking into the future, anticipating demand and competition for product(s), considering the other constraints and influences which may affect business growth and, so, developing a means of realizing opportunities whilst managing threats. Strategic planning enables facilities to be managed pro-actively.

An organization's strategic plan will be more achievable if it takes account of the vision and aspirations of all its sections. Wide involvement in the strategic planning process, rather than senior management simply dictating policies, can help to generate feelings of ownership as well as ensuring completeness. Input from operational departments can enhance responsiveness and flexibility of organizations to changing demand, by using all staff to identify opportunities – thus, enhancing competitiveness.

Service operations, therefore, have a 'bottom up' contribution to make to the strategic planning process as well as a 'top down' responsibility to translate strategic decisions into reality.

The mission statement

Before any detailed planning can take place, it is first necessary to identify:

● the mission of the organization
● its objectives (i.e. how it intends to achieve its mission).

In the past, many organizations have developed in a fairly haphazard manner, success has often been associated more with companies which could consistently meet customers' changing needs, adapting their service packages in an evolutionary manner. As organizations grow, it is important that all members of the organization remain aware of how the product they are involved in is changing and that they are in no doubt as to the overall objectives of the organization in which they work. Hence, the value of mission statements – enabling staff and all other stakeholders to understand the direction of the organization.

Organizations normally adopt one of several basic competitive missions. They can:

● compete on quality
● be a low cost provider always competing on price
● be a distinctive provider, concentrating on product or service differentiation
● concentrate effort by market segmentation (i.e. develop a range of different products or services for particular segments).

Within the context of the hotel business, the mission could be to provide:

- hotel services and facilities which delight customers
- the best hotel services in the country
- a friendly and welcoming environment to which guests will wish to return.

The strategy-making process

Planning and formulating strategy involves not only identifying the mission, but also putting this mission in the context of the organization. A common approach to identifying the current position of an organization is to apply a 'SWOT' analysis, relating to:

- Strengths.
- Weaknesses.
- Opportunities.
- Threats.

The attributes currently prominent of each of these must be identified and reconciled, together with the mission and any key social responsibilities and objectives that the organization has (e.g. provision of good working environment). This process should lead to the definition of:

- the nature of the products and services to be provided
- the nature of the markets to be served
- the manner in which these defined markets will be served.

The strategy must be determined in the light of the physical and financial resources available. A business policy must then be determined which establishes:

- the allocation of these resources

- the most appropriate organizational structure and information system to support them
- the human resource management philosophy, in terms of developing individuals
- the standards and performance measures
- the leadership style to be adopted.

Some possible business objectives for an hotel might be to:

- increase profitability and earnings per share each year in order to expand the business
- treat employees in such a way that they have every opportunity to perform their jobs to maximum effect
- always act with integrity.

The implications of these sample objectives, with respect to facilities management, can be seen in Table 2.2.

Strategic alliances and partnerships

Within the business policy, there may be a recognition of the fact that mutual benefit may be derived from developing some sort of agreement or 'strategic alliance' with another organization. This other organization could be an important supplier, a customer or even a competitor. It may be, for example that by sharing resources, two hotels could each derive greater benefit from their marketing budgets, or that by agreeing to somehow modify the product, the hotel can reach a long-term agreement. Strategic alliances might be used to protect current business in some way.

The benefits of strategic alliances might include economies of scale, risk diversification, increased market potential or innovation. Strategic alliances are often seen as essential in major new ventures such as international initiatives and, more recently, in the UK some such alliances have been formalized in partnership agreements.

Table 2.2 Examples of business objectives and their implications for the facilities manager

Objective	Implication for the facilities manager
To increase profitability and earnings per share each year in order to expand the business	Costs related to physical assets will come second only to staffing costs in the life of an hotel Facilities must be managed profitably, within the context of the mission statement and other objectives If buildings are considered to have a life span of 40–50 years, there might come a time when the facilities manager wants to move premises, expand or otherwise modify them, meanwhile, planned and running maintenance, cleaning and refurbishment all need to be managed in a way which achieves the right balance between: • ensuring that accommodation always meets the required standards • reducing room stock (or space available) for let, whilst maintenance activities are completed The right balance is needed of: • in-house and contract staff, energy management, customer control, full service and self-service • meeting guests' needs • considering employee needs
To treat employees in such a way that they have every opportunity to perform their jobs to maximum effect	The need to provide good recruitment, selection, training, supervision, working conditions and working environment, appropriate tools and materials, and opportunities for self-development Overall objectives – to provide the means and the motivation for employees to be able to and want to continually improve the way they and their colleagues perform their jobs
To always act with integrity	This relates to the business ethics, values and culture of the organization, in relation to staff, customers, suppliers, shareholders, the local community and any other stakeholders in the business

The product

Having established the strategy of the hotel and the facilities, it is then useful to consider exactly what is 'the product' on offer to customers and who are the customers.

As was shown in Chapter 1, the product offered by hotels includes physical or tangible elements (e.g. the space, the furniture and the heating), but it also comprises intangible elements (e.g. security and a feeling of well-being). These intangible elements identify the provision of hotel accommodation as a 'service industry'.

Therefore, the product or 'service package' (a more descriptive term) bought by guests comprises a number of elements and it is against these elements that customers will judge its value. These elements are summarized in Figure 2.1.

The actual facilities and services provided are obviously going to depend on the particular hotel and the customers it

Figure 2.1 The product or 'service package'.

aims to cater for. For example, secretarial facilities will not form part of a service package targeted at family holiday makers, whereas a cartoon themed guest room might.

Characteristics of service industries

Hotels clearly fall into the category of a service industry and these industries can be identified as having the following characteristics:

- They are labour intensive.
- There is a high level of customer participation and the service cannot happen without the customer (e.g. an hotel bedroom can be produced ready for occupation, but until a customer arrives, no service can take place).
- The service cannot be stored (e.g. a room not let tonight is a wasted or perishable resource).
- Production and consumption of the service element are simultaneous. A customer is greeted, directed to the room, served early morning tea – in each case, the customer is a necessary resource and the intangible service element (verbal or non-verbal communication) takes place only when the customer is present and at a moment in time.
- Output of the service element is difficult to measure. Was the customer greeted with a smile? Was information given courteously? Did staff give the impression of a desire to please?
- At least part of the service package is intangible (e.g. the environment in which the service contact is made, the ambience of the room and the nature of the service contact).

Implications of these service characteristics to the facilities manager

These characteristics have important implications as far as the management of the service package is concerned and, taking the characteristics point by point, implications are identified in Table 2.3.

The service package produced in service industries comprises:

- the physical item
- the environment in which the service contact occurs
- the nature of the actual service contact.

In an hotel:

- the **physical item** will include the hotel and its facilities
- the **environment** will include the comfort conditions (e.g. heating, ventilation and aesthetics)
- the **nature of the service contact** will be the intangible element, represented perhaps by the attitude of the receptionist greeting a guest, the attentiveness of the waiter taking an order or the astuteness of the conference organizer in advising the potential client (although these actions do not produce anything tangible, they can have considerable impact on the perceived quality and nature of the accommodation package).

Facilities management is concerned with each of these elements. It has direct relevance to the physical item and the environment as it is a property-based discipline and emphasizes the need for strategic management of all physical assets. To manage these elements effectively, techniques applied to manufacturing industries (e.g. work study, materials management and value analysis) have relevance. By providing an effective work environment for staff (e.g. ensuring the receptionist can comfortably assess up-to-date booking information, room availability and pricing, and see the customer all at the same time), facilities management also impacts on the third element, that is, the nature of the service contact.

Table 2.3 Service characteristics and their implications

Characteristic	Implication
Labour intensive	Personnel functions need to be well developed and recruitment, training, interpersonal skills, safety and motivation are important
Participation of the customer	The location of the accommodation must be easily accessible, unless: • the accommodation is moveable (e.g. marquees) • provision is made to transport customers to the service point (e.g. hotel taxis) Customers must be identified as a resource, they may need directing (training) in the use of the product Layout may need to take account of customer control and their movement through the facility
Service cannot be stored	It may be necessary to reduce or increase the capacity* round fluctuations of demand (e.g. shift work, part-time staff) and/or attempt to control demand (e.g. advertising and marketing)
Simultaneous production and consumption of the service element	Quality is difficult to manage and record. Restricting the numbers of 'contact' staff and concentrating training in customer contact skills to these may be feasible Non-contact or 'back of house' staff then would be less involved in the intangible service element Automation is a means of affecting control
Output is difficult to measure	This can be measured by customers and recorded by surveys By monitoring, 'spot checks' can be made on output and indirect results measured (e.g. number of return clients)
Intangible element of the package	Difficulties in setting, measuring and controlling standards and services cannot be patented The market share must be captured quickly Increasing automation is one effective way of standardizing the package Intensive training and retraining of staff is vital

*Facilities (including staffing) within an organization which allow it to achieve a given output

Core and non-core business

An hotel may have many facilities and functions available to guests, ranging from a full à la carte menu and extensive wine list, and leisure facilities to an early call system and personal laundry service. Its staff may include beauticians, receptionists and porters. It may cater for a conference trade, those using wheel-chairs and foreign visitors, but in the vast majority of hotels, whoever the target customer might be, the 'core' business is the letting of guest rooms.

To put the value of accommodation into perspective, research by Howarth Consulting (1991) showed that in UK hotels:

- room sales represent approximately 40–50 per cent of all sales
- recent room occupancy rates average 60–70 per cent
- property occupation and maintenance cost about 3–4 per cent of total turnover
- energy costs 3–4 per cent of total turnover.

Estimates by the English Tourist Board show that about one-third of money spent by tourists is on accommodation.

The core business of an organization is that part of the business which is critical to the success of the organization and without which the business cannot successfully operate. The core business relates to the core competencies on which the organization's on-going success and survival is based. From this core business, there may be periphery services (e.g. the bar or the photocopying service) which operate at varying profit margins. In the case of hotels, therefore, the core business will usually relate to letting of space and the non-core business to the related services.

Figure 2.2 shows the responses given by hoteliers to the question, 'What is your core business?'.

If the rooms represent the core business of hotels, there can be no doubt that the management of these facilities plays a

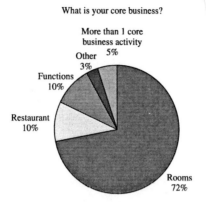

Figure 2.2 Core business in hotels.

critical role in the success of the enterprise. This core business comprises three 'core elements', without which the hotel cannot function:

1   the building and its interior or environment
2   the guestroom and its facilities and appearance
3   the reception and sales section.

Non-core elements are the additional elements which may or may not be offered by a particular hotel (e.g. games rooms, trouser presses and room service).

Market segmentation

Normally, an hotel's customer base comprises a predominant type(s) of customers who share similar characteristics. They can be grouped into particular market segments which are relevant in planning the marketing strategy and enabling the hotel to target its facilities and services.

By identifying certain groups or market segments, the detailed needs of those individuals can be recognized and the service package suitably enhanced. The core elements can be designed round those needs and non-core elements selected specifically to meet the needs of the market segments to be targeted.

Segmentation may be by attributes, buying behaviour, type of organization or source of business. Market segments which might be considered include:

- business men
- business women
- weekend break
- over 60s
- economy
- mid-week break
- disabled
- cultural interest
- family
- long-term stays
- foreign
- sport interest
- conference
- school parties
- air travellers
- retired
- tourists
- under 30s
- walkers
- naturalists.

The market segments targeted will depend largely on the location and the mission of the hotel. Segmenting markets also helps an organization to monitor competitive activity, compare success rates and determine its competitive edge. Business efficiency can be improved by analysing the volume of business attributable to each segment.

In determining market segments to target, the following aspects should be considered.

- Size – is the segment large enough to j
  marketing effort?
- Identity – can this segment clearly be discriminate~
  other segments?
- Relevance – is the segment relevant to the particular ethos,
  facilities, services, location or capability of the hotel?
- Access – is it feasible to communicate with that segment in
  a cost-effective way?
- Profitability – what benefits would the hotel derive from
  this segment in preference to another and would this
  represent a good return on resources?

By targeting specific segments of the population, the service
package can be made more attractive to those individuals and
the marketing of the package can become more focused.
Through the service package and its marketing, the strategic
planning of facilities management can have a two-pronged
approach to setting the following objectives.

1 Objectives directed at operations, including setting
  policies for:
  - quality
  - productivity
  - outsourcing
  - computerization
  - the working environment
  - revenue maximization
  - vendor rating, procurement and materials
    management
  - human resource management.
2 Objectives directed at marketing, including:
  - market segmentation and research
  - new product development
  - promotions and advertising
  - product packaging
  - pricing.

Customer focus

Having initially identified the market segment(s) to be targeted in an hotel, the next stage is to thoroughly analyse the needs of those potential customers. There are obviously advantages to customers in dealing with organizations which understand and recognize their needs and, as far as the hotel is concerned, the business obviously relies on customers.

Customers are not adversaries or intrusions to put staff under pressure or upset comfortable working routines! In a service operation, particularly a profit-making one, it is essential and often costly to attract customers. It is five times cheaper to retain an existing customer than to attract a new one. An hotel needs to develop a good reputation, encourage customer loyalty and encourage repeat custom. When a good service experience is enjoyed, customers tell other people. Then the customer base, profits, business and sales are likely to grow. When a bad service operation occurs, customers may not only not return but may tell ten times as many people. The bottom line is that in a competitive market, the hotel will only get the business if the customer chooses to give it.

Everyone is a salesperson

Everyone working in an hotel – from the engineer to the manager – can be considered as a potential salesperson and is responsible for selling the organization and its service package. Staff 'sell' to customers in every word and action. The relationship created between staff and customers creates a unique customer care opportunity and, in a profit-oriented business, an opportunity for increasing volume of sales. This relationship may or may not impress or delight the customer, may or may not encourage the customer to sample a wider range of the facilities and services available to him or her, and it may or may not encourage repeat business or recommendation to other potential customers. The attitude and approach of staff can have a negative effect on reputation and sales.

At a basic level, 'selling' is concerned with customer care – making the customer feel welcome, comfortable, relaxed and at ease and satisfying his or her needs by providing the experience, services and benefits for which he or she has paid. 'Selling' is about making the customer feel valued and making him or her feel like the most important person in the organization.

Product knowledge and product analysis

All staff involved in the provision and delivery of a service package need to have a comprehensive product knowledge. This is important as it enables:

- more effective management and provision
- more effective advertising, promotion and selling
- describes the service package effectively to the customer and conveys an accurate mental picture, particularly over the telephone or in promotional brochures
- the quality standards of the service package being promoted to be evaluated
- comparison with competitors' products and services
- identification of strengths which can be maximized and improved and weaknesses which can be eliminated
- monitoring of performance in terms of volume of sales and viability of the whole and constituent parts
- analysis of the cost of provision
- more effective staff briefing.

Having product knowledge is part of the customer care philosophy. Being able to answer customers' questions easily and correctly in a helpful manner conveys a caring attitude and impacts on the customers' total experience of the service package.

knowledge may be imparted through briefing ses-
os, conducted tours, sampling and documentation.
nd competitions keep staff up-to-date and on their
toes as well as refreshing their memories. Staff product
knowledge must be updated when changes occur.

Who are the customers?

The following are typical questions which hotel managers or
front office managers might ask to gain some insight into the
characteristics of their 'external' customers.

- What is their socio-economic group, gender, occupation
  and income level?
- Where do they originate from – in terms of country, county
  or area and location of company/organization?
- From what source is their custom generated? Is it through
  travel agents, tour operators, central reservations or agency,
  business house or company? Is it corporate or individual?
- What is the lead time between reservations being made and
  reservation dates?
- What proportion of potential customers cancel or do not
  show?
- What is the reason for their stay?
- How long do they stay? What is the average length of stay
  per month or how many guests stay – one, two, three, four
  or five nights in a month?
- When do they come – at the weekend, during the week, in
  spring, in summer, at Christmas?
- How much is the average spend by each type of guest and
  by nationality? What is the amount spent by tour guests
  compared with other individuals?
- What method of payment do customers use – foreign cur-
  rency, travellers cheques, cheques, eurocheques, credit card,
  cash or transfer to ledger?
- How many bad debts are incurred?

● Are customers satisfied? What do they like or dislike, what do they complain about?

Management can never know enough about their customers. Much of this information can be extracted from existing records periodically and used to monitor changes in each element. IT makes graphic compilation much easier and aids comparisons over a period of time.

Guest or customer history

It is usual in many hotels, particularly the large chain operations, to maintain a guest history. This is especially useful in providing continuity in the treatment of regular customers. Thus, a record containing dates of stays, rooms used or preferred, total bills and likes and dislikes (e.g. in terms of food, drinks, types of pillows, duvet or traditional bedding) provides a useful database. Most front office software includes a guest history facility which can be expensive to maintain manually. It allows returning guests to be recognized on reservation and greeted appropriately on registration. Some hotels have separate, more informal, registration areas for regular customers which also assures a speedier check in.

Customer records or profiles may also be maintained on corporate clients and on conference and banqueting clients for sales and marketing purposes. Such records may contain information on the key decision-makers in an organization, the customer's buying power, volume and the type of business purchased or used, when purchased and for whom and the details of the products and services of competitors that these customers use.

Managing customers

In service operations, the customer can be seen as another resource to be managed. Customers need to be managed in re and evacuation of the building. They also need ___ informed of how to access and use hotel facilities and services without being embarrassed, patronized or frustrated. A new guest entering a five star hotel for the first time might feel overawed and unsure and will need help in operating within the hotel system without being made to feel foolish.

Customers also need managing when they:

- are involved in the production of the service by providing their own labour (e.g. carrying their own luggage, making their own bed or using the self-service minibar in their room)
- need to pass through a number of stages in a prescribed manner (e.g. a guest arriving and registering at an hotel)
- need guidance on appropriate behaviour (e.g. when entering a restaurant for the first time, customers need to know whether to wait to be seated or seat themselves and whether it is waiter service or self-service buffet)
- are expected to provide feedback as part of the quality assurance and monitoring process (e.g. reporting faults, complaining or commenting on standards).

The most appropriate means of communication to inform the customer effectively must be carefully considered, whether this be orally by staff, written in a personalized way or on notices and signs.

Customer care

Customer care is an important part of the service package and can be an effective marketing and promotional tool to help an organization to increase its profits. Good customer care needs to occur as a matter of course and is achieved essentially by well-motivated and trained staff.

Customer care is basically an attitude or state of mind which must originate from senior management and cascade throughout the operation, focusing on the customer as the most important person in the operation. Customer care will only work if all staff are enthusiastic and committed to it and all pull in the same direction.

Customer satisfaction is essential if an organization is to gain a competitive edge in the market place. Customer care is about adding value and it becomes meaningless if the service package does not satisfy the customer in the first place. Customer care is about the interaction between individuals in the organization and customers. Those contact staff involved in the interface with customers must have a customer-oriented approach. The customer's first impressions of an organization will have a great impact on the relationship which they subsequently develop with contact staff. Contact staff are the organization to the customer. Customers are all individuals with an individual name which should be used at every opportunity.

One airline which adopts a strategy of putting people first suggests that the way staff are managed strongly influences how they react with customers and that customers can see what management style an organization adopts by the service received from employees. In a 'transparent organization', company philosophy is reflected in the attitudes of staff, their enthusiasm for the job, pride in themselves and in their work, in their appearance, and in their product knowledge and professionalism.

Enthusiasm is catching and bringing a smile to a customer's face can only be done by another smiling face. One hotel has even put a mirror in reception so that as staff look at themselves they will smile. Staff need to be attentive, good listeners and observers and able to ask the right questions to ascertain customers' needs and requirements. They also need to be helpful in any way possible at any time and provide relevant information without intruding or interfering. Attention to detail is important – 'little things' make a qualitative difference.

New customers will have a service expectation and some

r expectations than others. If they have a bad
are likely to think that this is the norm and
rily be impressed with the other elements of
the service package. Staff must start to see things from the
customer's point of view. Sampling the service package will
allow staff to step into customers' shoes. However, staff must
be supported by the organization if they are to succeed in
maintaining a consistently high standard of customer service.
Customer care training is essential and adequate resourcing
and possibly some kind of incentive scheme may enhance
endeavours.

Research shows that for customers to experience satisfaction on a continual basis, the total package (including tangible
and intangible elements) must be appropriate to their needs.
The tangible or procedural dimensions include not only the
physical assets of the hotel, but also efficiency, receipt of correct documentation, speed of service, the quality standard of
the physical elements of the service package, customer feedback
and the communications systems. The intangible or convivial
dimensions include staff attitudes, attentiveness, body
language, tone of voice, friendliness, problem-solving skills and
enthusiasm. All these dimensions should be part of the
customer care strategy and must be supported by feedback
from customers and training.

Measuring customer satisfaction

Ensuring customer satisfaction is one of an hotel's most
important activities and, unless customer loyalty can be
retained, it will not sustain its business and its long-term future
is uncertain. Customer satisfaction is at the heart of retaining
loyalty and is the responsibility of all staff within an organization. Customer satisfaction is about meeting or exceeding
customer expectations. Customer satisfaction is a continuous
process covering the whole experience – from hotel enquiry

and selection to purchasing and experiencing the service package, and on to follow up and repeat purchase.

An organization may believe that it is satisfying its customers, but how does it know? In a service industry, management have the advantage of direct access to their end customers, unlike the position in manufacturing industries where the makers of the product often never come face-to-face with their product users.

By talking directly to customers, feedback can be obtained in specific aspects of the whole package. Contact staff should be trained to be sensitive to the changing needs, expectations and satisfaction levels of the customers with whom they deal. These staff must then be encouraged to pass on this information to those in a position to respond. If an hotel manager or an appointed member of staff conducted even a couple of informal customer interviews per day, a valuable database would soon be built up. A written record of such interviews is necessary as the memory is fickle and only by developing this information base can trends be spotted and forecasts made.

Other ways of measuring customer satisfaction include:

- monitoring how far the organization's quality standards are being achieved
- undertaking guest tests, whereby regular guests or other people are appointed to sample and test systems and procedures and give feedback
- reviewing all identified problems and complaints regularly, looking for patterns and trying to identify causes and then taking action to avoid repetition in the future
- staff sampling the service package, giving them the chance to experience the customer's perspective and to develop a better product knowledge
- conducting customer surveys by means of a customer satisfaction questionnaire (to design an appropriate questionnaire, focus on specific areas for review which can then be piloted on a small scale and amended prior to wider usage – see the sample questionnaire in Figure 2.3).

Burton Hotel Customer Questionnaire

We at The Burton Hotel try constantly to improve the services we offer to our guests and would be grateful for your help in this process. Could you please answer these questions.

Your name will not be recorded with the answers.

(Please tick relevant response or state reason as shown.)

1 Is this your first visit to this hotel?   Yes/No

If no, when was your last visit? (Please state) ....

    Do you notice any changes?   Yes/No

    If yes, please state their nature ....

2 How did you choose this hotel?

3 Where did you find out about this hotel?

4 Is it up to your expectations?   Yes/No

    If not, why not? (Please state) ....

5 What is most important to you when staying at an hotel? (Please state) ....

....

6 Are you relaxed here?   Yes/No

7 Do you feel you have been treated courteously?   Yes/No

8 Are there any other facilities you would have liked to be available at this hotel?   Yes/No

If yes, please state...

9 What do you feel about the decor? (Please state)...

....

10 How would you describe the other guests staying at the hotel?...

....

Thank you for your help.

Figure 2.3 Customer questionnaire.

Results from customer satisfaction surveys sho checked against other information (e.g. comments rec from suppliers or conference delegates). The avid compla .cr is more likely to complete such questionnaires, but any suggestions should be treated as opportunities and a mechanism must exist for reviewing and, where necessary, acting on comments from such questionnaires.

By utilizing the resource of direct access to customers, particularly through their contact with staff, hotels have the chance to respond rapidly to external opportunities. If they can monitor changing needs *and* respond to them rapidly, they may achieve a competitive advantage and remain successful. Having the ability to develop new service packages and market them quickly calls for well-trained and flexible staff. Such a responsive organization is often referred to as a 'fast cycle' organization.

At one time, competitiveness meant reducing costs, perhaps by rescheduling, mechanization or by finding a cheaper supplier. It can no longer be achieved purely through cost-cutting exercises. Organizations have to be able to respond rapidly to market demands. The restructuring of organizations, which has been influenced by the changes discussed in Chapter 1, has made all employees more aware of, and more responsive to, the needs of the customer. The Investors in People standard stresses the importance of all employees recognizing the mission of the organization and, in the case of hotels, the significance of customers.

Organizational needs

In this chapter, in considering organizational strategy, the nature of the service package and the customer, a number of key issues have been emphasized. The requirements for the hotel to be sensitive to customer needs, responsive to change, adaptable and in search of continuous improvement are evident. The key to all these issues is the staff. Hotels will need staff who are:

- enthusiastic
- committed
- self-motivated
- capable of using their initiative with the minimum of supervision
- in possession of good interpersonal skills
- able to communicate well, working in a consultative manner
- flexible and adaptable
- able to cope with and initiate change
- able to rise to the challenge
- creative, innovative and entrepreneurial
- skilled at problem-solving
- able to organize.

In turn, organizations will have to accommodate staff who are more aware of changing work and career patterns, who expect to have multiple careers and who desire variety, autonomy, opportunities for continuous professional development and a balanced and more comfortable lifestyle. The human resource is discussed more fully in Chapter 6.

Meeting customer requirements

The following questions (MCI, 1993) are essential in determining how a service operation is meeting its customer requirements now and into the future.

- Do you know what your customers' needs and requirements are or do you only think you do?
- Do you assume that they need what you give them, when you give it to them and in the form that you give it them?
- Has anything changed recently which may affect their requirements?
- Can you improve the service package which you provide for them in some way?

- Do you know what your customers want from your service package?
- How can you exceed customer satisfaction and create customer commitment?
- How can you anticipate future customer needs and keep one step ahead?
- How can you best organize and use your resources to provide ever-increasing customer satisfaction and ever-improving value for money?
- How can you achieve the above at the same time as reducing costs and improving profit margins?
- Do you carry out reviews with your customers revisiting these questions on a regular basis?

It is worth considering how staff at all levels can be empowered to contribute to the process of actively seeking customers' perspectives and feelings towards the service package to enable the organization to be responsive.

References and further reading

Armistead, C., Johnston, R. and Slack, N. (1988) The strategic determinants of service productivity. In *Management of Service Operations* (R. Johnston, ed.). Prentice Hall.

Collier, D. (1987) *Services Management*. Prentice Hall.

English Tourist Board (1996) *English Hotel Occupancy Survey*.

Howarth Consulting (1991) *United Kingdom Hotel Industry*. Howarth Consulting.

Management Charter Initiative (MCI) (1993) Module 9: Everyone's a Customer. *Effective Manager*. MCI.

Thompson, J.L. (1990) *Strategic Management, Awareness and Change*. Chapman and Hall.

Worthing, D. (1995) Strategic Property Management Facilities Management Handbook (A. Spedding, ed.).

3
The physical assets – the building envelope

Aims and objectives

This chapter aims to:

- consider the design and development of buildings
- identify the key elements of the building envelope and their implications for the facilities manager
- analyse the environmental services within a building, their selection and management
- consider the elements and principles of an integrated design
- consider the maintenance, safety, security and welfare implications of the working environment.

Property valuation

As has been shown in Chapter 1, facilities management is a property-based discipline, its objective being to achieve efficiency of operation. If an hotel is located in the 'right' place, has good access and is well-designed, -furnished, -maintained and -cleaned, the use of space can be maximized. The facilities will encourage sales and working conditions will enable staff to operate effectively.

Without the facilities, the operation cannot exist. They represent a major capital resource and this value should be monitored. Property valuation can inform decisions regarding income targets, future development or sale, and indeed the judgement as to whether the hotel business is the right one to be in. Would more income be generated by selling the hotel and going into some other business?

Without knowledge of the current value of their property, it is impossible for the owner or manager to judge performance. In a survey of hotels (Jones, 1997) in the West Midlands, 74 per cent of respondents said the property was freehold – its value, therefore, must be one of the criteria used in measuring the success of the operation. In addition, knowledge of trends in the property values in the locality can also be useful. If property values are declining or rising less, there may be marketing implications for the future. Is the locality still right to attract the market segment targeted by the hotel?

The building and the other physical assets of a hospitality operation can represent a considerable competitive advantage.

Elements of a building

The elements of a building can be identified as:

- the site
- the structure
- the fittings.

In terms of lifespans, the site is, of course, everlasting. The structure, in the UK, would be considered to have a lifespan of around 40 years (though its external finish or cladding might be changed 2 or 3 times during that period). The fittings and services may last 7–15 years according to Brand (1994), being replaced due to obsolescence or failure. The importance of site selection and structure design can, of course, be appreciated with respect to the long-lasting repercussions.

The site

The site for an hotel is always going to be a key factor in its on-going success. The lifespan of buildings is considered to be around 40 years and the environment immediately surrounding the site and how it may change in the future need to be considered. The site might be the precise size of the building structure or it might comprise acres of land. It has physical and other environmental characteristics which will influence the structure of the operation and probably the success of the establishment, as shown in Table 3.1. It can also have a significant effect on energy efficiency.

The structure

The structure of a conventional building comprises:

- foundations (e.g. footings and pile – the type being dependent on geophysical aspects and building shape)
- walls, either framed (e.g. timber, steel, concrete with infill panels of glass-reinforced concrete, glass-reinforced plastic and brick – possibly with an external cladding) or load bearing (e.g. concrete and masonry)
- roof (flat or ridged).

Prefabricated sections, pods or modules may however be used. Prefabrication has benefits for cost and speed of construction.

The structure imparts physical and psychological qualities. It must be firm to resist forces of compression and tension (e.g. gravity, water, wind and loads). Loads may be live (e.g. furniture, snow loading and people) or 'dead' (e.g. gravity and the weight of the building itself). Most elements of the building are designed to transfer these loads through the structure to the ground. Physical qualities will be achieved by a combination of the characteristics of the materials used and their configuration. The style of structure can have considerable influence on the final flexibility of use of the finished building.

Table 3.1 Aspects of site and their influence on managing the facility

Site characteristic	Influence on management of facility
Geographical location	Proximity to consumers and need for transport
	Access and need for adaptation to meet particular customer needs
	Climate – affecting demand patterns and energy consumption
	Availability of labour and supplies and lead time
	Local planning regulations
Aspect (and other structures in the vicinity)	Amount of sun, shade and wind
Geophysical	Bearing capacity of land
	Suitability for building
	Type of structure and foundations
	Drainage
	Access
	Landscaping and use of adjoining land
Dimensions	Shape and size of building and adjoining land
Pollutants (e.g. noise, vibration, carbon, sulphur, and visual)	Aesthetic desirability of site Foundations, structure and materials
Other structures	Aesthetic qualities
	Demand

Psychological qualities (e.g. appearance of comfort, efficiency or informality) can be affected by design, shape and the materials used.

The fittings and services

The fittings of a building include:

- partitions
- window frames
- doors
- gutters
- water and sanitary fittings
- heating and electrical items, including IT cabling
- finishing items (e.g. architraves and skirtings).

The fittings represent the more flexible items of the building and may be removed or modified without affecting the integrity of the building itself.

Planning, design and construction

In building design, as in the design of any other item, different systems can operate. One such design process can be seen in craft industries (e.g. pottery), where design and construction go hand-in-hand. The design evolves with the construction and is modified as construction progresses and new approaches are visualized. This is possible since the designer, the end user and the constructor are the same person.

At the opposite end of the design spectrum is what is called the 'rational network' (see Figure 3.1).

The user might not even exist when the product is first considered. The client and the designer must endeavour to predict the user requirements. They must try to satisfy the needs of the maximum number of future users. This design

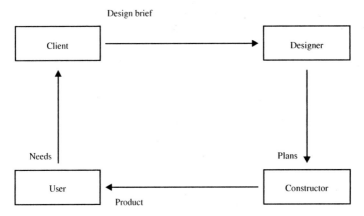

Figure 3.1 Rational design network.

process is the norm, when considering large public buildings. The client may be an hotel group, the designer is the architect and the architect's team and the constructor usually consists of a number of contractors. Inevitably, when a building is constructed, it is rare for all of the users to be satisfied with all of the building, which is likely to be stereotyped in the hope of satisfying most of the people most of the time.

The facilities manager, can play a particularly useful role in the rational network by clearly identifying user needs and by ensuring sufficient flexibility is incorporated into the design to satisfy changes in those needs.

Planning

A brief outline of the design phase of a building is as follows. The client reaches a decision that there is a need to build. This problem realization stage leads the client to consult an architect. At the first consultation, the architect would not want the client to outline any definite plans. The architect needs to be briefed on 'the problem' and will need to discuss the client's general ideas. A site may or may not have been found at this phase, but detailed planning cannot occur until this element has been acquired.

The feasibility study may have been completed by the client, or the architect may have been commissioned to make a study. Some of the aspects to be considered in such a feasibility study are shown in Table 3.2.

In order to foresee needs, the facilities manager might organize a planning team, comprising representatives of different disciplines of future users. In an hotel, for example, a food and beverage specialist might be invited to join the team when catering issues are being considered, the executive housekeeper

Table 3.2 Building feasibility study

Key issues	Examples of elements
The consumer identification	Local population, current and predicted trends, tourism and commerce
	Population type (e.g. age, health and wealth)
	Accessibility of the site
	Communication links of the area
	Competition
Total capital costs	Site
	Design and construction costs
	Equipment and furnishings
	Pre-opening costs (e.g. stock)
	Insurance, rates and rent
	Debtors
Predicted return on capital and running costs	Analysis of expenditure
	Payback periods
	Replacement cycles
	Cash flow

or front office manager at other appropriate times. The objectives of the planning team are to ensure a comprehensive and appropriate brief by representing the future users of the proposed building.

Design

The design phase follows problem identification and briefing, though the distinction is not clear cut. There are four basic aspects:

1 brief finalization
2 analysis of requirements
3 synthesis of plans
4 implementation of plans.

Brief finalization

The architect may be responsible for the completion of the feasibility study. Certainly, the architect must analyse the requirements identified by the client and also the future needs of building users. In the 40-year life of the building, changes of function may well occur and the needs of users change. Consideration must be given to such flexibility, if the building is to be successful. For example, in recent years in the UK, hospital properties in city centre locations have been sold to businesses moving into the cities, whilst hospitals have moved out to green field sites.

In some cases, the client's planning horizon and need for a speedy completion, may dictate a much less permanent structure.

Analysis

In the planning and construction of large public buildings, the design network involves the client, the designer, the constructor and the user. Since the users, as individuals, might not have been identified yet, the client and the architect must predict their needs. In some instances, the rational design network may become further sophisticated. Standard packages have been developed, in the interests of speed and economy.

The users of a building are not just the sports people in a leisure complex or the customers in a restaurant. The building users include staff, spectators, suppliers, contractors and fire-fighters. User requirements can be considered as:

1   individual needs, including:
    ● physical needs (e.g. shelter, heat, light, food, sanita-
      tion, sleeping facilities, ventilation, security and safety)
    ● functional needs to enable proposed activities to be car-
      ried out (e.g. furniture and equipment)
    ● psychological needs (e.g. privacy, efficiency, companion-
      ship and status)
2   group needs, including:
    ● social interaction requirements
    ● space for business transactions
    ● social functions.

In assessing both group and individual needs, changes in fashion, attitude and the standards required must be considered. All the identified needs must be analysed and their implications interpreted by the architect in the form of plans for the new building.

In developing plans, the architect must aim to allow individual and group activities to be carried out:

● economically
● conveniently
● efficiently
● comfortably.

To achieve this, ergonomic theory is applied (see 'Ergonomic aspects'). This will indicate, among other things, how much space is required for different activities.

Synthesis

From the data collected at the synthesis stage, the architect will start drawing conclusions and developing plans. At this stage, it is the architect's aim to offer a variety of possibilities to the client. Testing, checking and re-designing work will occur, as the client and architect meet to discuss the plans. These plans are only at the sketch plan stage.

By this stage, the architect is likely to have involved others in the team (e.g. engineers and a quantity surveyor to advise on practicalities and economic matters, respectively). Plans proposed must meet legal requirements and provisional planning permission may be applied for.

The architect now has information with respect to building users and their activities. Legal, safety and cost constraints must be considered at the same time as ensuring that the required activities can take place efficiently and comfortably. Also to be considered are:

- numbers of people
- types of individual activity
- types of group activity
- timing and places of activities
- the implications of different activities (e.g. noise created or quiet needed)
- how activities coincide.

The effect that social and economic trends may have on activities in the future (e.g. the concept of 'hot desks' or shared offices) has been applied to some office spaces in commercial environments – users only use the space for limited periods in the week and others can be scheduled to use the space at different times. Room configurations need to meet individual, group and operational needs.

Ergonomic aspects

To achieve user comfort, ergonomic theory is applied. Ergonomics looks at the characteristics of people in order to develop equipment and procedures that are suited to these characteristics. It involves an examination of people's capabilities and limitations. Broadly, there are four aspects involved in ergonomics.

1   **Anthropometrics** This involves measurement of average human dimensions for specified groups (e.g. nurses, car drivers or the adult population as a whole). Dimensions available are virtually unlimited and include heights, arm lengths, eye levels and finger lengths. Such information is used by many sectors, including furniture manufacturers, industrial workplace designers and architects. The information allows the architect to specify dimensions of doors, windows, work surfaces, steps and any other building element to achieve functional, comfortable, convenient, efficient and economic design.

2   **Kinetics** This is a study of the muscles of the human body and their use. Architects need to consider how the user's body will be positioned and which muscles will be used when undertaking any activity for which the building is being designed. For example, if a user is moving a heavy object (e.g. lifting a suitcase onto a stand in a guestroom), there needs to be enough space to allow larger muscles in the arms and legs to be used in preference to smaller back muscles.

3   **Applied physiology** Human physiological data also needs to be applied to building design. The architect needs an understanding of people's physical requirements in terms of fresh air, temperature, humidity and lighting. The architect should aslo take into account the effect of noise, odour, mechanical vibration, visual effects (including colour, pattern, shape and light intensities), the need for

sustenance and sanitary facilities, and the effects of air movements and tactile qualities.

4 **Applied psychology** This is concerned with the human mental state and needs dependent on the activities carried out and on the specific user groups. Aspects to consider here include how much mental stimulation to create in an area or, conversely, how to achieve a restful and relaxing environment, and how to create an impression of informality, efficiency, opulence, tradition, intimacy or discipline. The mood created may need to be flexible in response to perceived needs. Different groups have different psychological needs and abilities and they vary in their motivation, concentration, learning patterns and interactive behaviour.

Applying ergonomic theory can, therefore, assist the architect in designing a practical and economic environment in which users will feel comfortable.

Room sizes and shapes

The usefulness of a room is affected by the shape and siteing of door and windows. These limit the size and arrangement of furniture and, therefore, the activities which can operate within the room. Space represents money and cannot be wasted, but adequate space must be available to achieve comfort.

As the synthesis stage progresses and as the architect develops room plans and layouts, a recommended schedule of furniture will also be prepared. This will be needed to help the client to assess the plans. Again, the needs of particular user groups will be considered (e.g. wheelchair users will require lateral transfer space beside beds and baths). Some large institutions use standard activity database material. Given the type of activity within a room, a standard recommended schedule of furniture is developed. Further than this, given the activity and component (e.g. activity: emptying or filling water jugs; component: a sink), component database information provides standard specifications for the defined components.

Details of the furniture schedule will form the basis of an asset register detailing all the physical assets over a given value within the establishment. The given value may be as little as £20, but it represents the sum of elements which must be maintained, serviced, insured or otherwise managed within the establishment. This information can inform the facilities manager on workloads and the overall scope of asset management and if kept up-to-date can assist in costing exercises (e.g. depreciation and replacement).

As a logical extension of component databases and through developments in building technology 'components' could now refer to composite units, such as a toilet or bathroom module consisting of a pre-specified package of toilet, cistern, washbasin, tiles and taps. Such prefabricated 'pods' or modules can be connected to the mains and fitted with relative speed and ease.

Actual room sizes and shapes will not only be dependent on the fittings, their dimensions and layout, but also on the shape and site of the building and the environment (e.g. a sea view), on the activities planned for that room and the ergonomic needs which have been identified. The needs of the disabled, for example, as well as the able-bodied should be considered. In the interest of economy, the architect will consider use of space carefully. Due to the multiplying effects of costs, even slight increases in room sizes are expensive. It may be possible to reduce room sizes, but not to reduce space availability. Two single rooms may take up 50 per cent more space than one twin room, yet the useable space may only be in the region of 20 per cent greater in the single room.

Space allocations must reflect market demand. Generally, more luxurious hotels have more space allocated to each customer than the lower grade hotels. Within an hotel, the ratio of single, twin, double or studio rooms must be based on data collected in the feasibility study. The architect will also need to consider standardization of room sizes within an hotel group. Significant economies can be made through standardisation and simplification of 'the product', such as through standardization of purchases and bulk purchasing as well as the simplification of the building process, which might involve the use of prefabricated sections or units.

Finally, the architect will be constrained in the design of the building by legal aspects, local bylaws and fire regulations. Building regulations, for example, cover:

- access and egress
- sanitary facilities
- audience or spectator seating.

Implementation

The presentation of final designs and plans to the client (in some cases, alternative proposals may be submitted) can be considered as the implementation stage. Data has been interpreted in plans and a proposal developed. If the client now chooses to alter the brief, work will have been wasted and the client will bear the cost. Working drawings are developed, so that, following acceptance of the plans, tenders can be invited, contracts made and building can commence. A summary of the design phase is given in Figure 3.2.

Construction

By the completion of the design phase, every part of the building has been detailed and costings calculated. Engineers and quantity surveyors will have joined the architect. Planning permission will have been applied for (in the UK, to comply with the Town and Country Planning Act 1954) and plans will also need the approval of other bodies, including the police, the fire authority and the Health and Safety Executive.

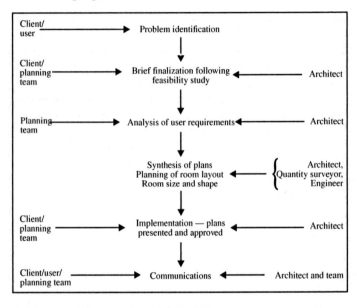

Figure 3.2 Summary of design phase.

Those providing services such as water, telecommunications, electricity and gas will also need to be contacted.

The bill of quantities, prepared by the quantity surveyor, provides the foundation of tender documents. A clerk of works will be appointed, with responsibility for inspecting and controlling work on site.

Construction processes vary, but once the land has been purchased the construction will need to be completed as quickly as possible, whilst complying with quality standards, to enable the capital spent to facilitate income generation. Concrete and piles and system building techniques are examples of processes used to allow speedy completion. In new economy hotels, system building techniques enable a complete hotel to be constructed in 20 weeks or less, following planning permission. Revenue is generated so much sooner than could be achieved by conventional building processes.

The three types of system building are panel, pod and complete module. The most common method is panel construction, whereby panels for each wall are factory-made and assembled on site. Modules enable the complete building to be made and assembled in the factory and transported to the site, whereas pods comprise units (e.g. the bathroom) to be factory-made and erected together with other panels. Apart from the speed of construction, this process also enables a much more consistent standard to be achieved for the chain hotels who may be opening premises in different parts of the country.

Commissioning

During the construction of the building, the client can plan its functioning. As building completion nears, orders for inventory may be placed and some staff recruitment, selection and preparatory training can occur. The commissioning teams, led by the facilities manager, would be aiming to have finishes and furnishings selected and fitted as soon as practicable. Once the building ownership passes to the client, it is important that business and income generation commences as soon as possible. To this end, the facilities manager will have an important role in organizing and coordinating the commissioning phase. All departments need to be encouraged to plan their part of the operation and ensure that preparations are complete to allow speedy functioning.

At the date of the handover, insurance liability for the building passes from the architect to the client. Following the handover of the building, there is a period of defects liability during which the architect should be informed of any defects and ensure that those occurring as a result of a deviation from the specification are made good.

The fittings

The many components within a building have different life expectancies. Wall coverings, for example, may be changed every 3 or 4 years, water and drainage systems may be expected to function for 15 years or more. This section considers the elements the building users will interface with most directly. In each case, possible performance attributes will be considered, specific types identified, the different characteristics analysed and selection criteria suggested.

Environmental services

Water

Water is used in buildings for:

- personal hygiene
- culinary purposes
- cleaning processes
- manufacturing processes
- heating systems
- fire-fighting
- health and leisure pursuits.

Water enters the building through mains, under sufficient pressure to meet fire-fighting requirements (supplemented by a pump in high-rise buildings). It may then pass through a softening plant, designed to reduce the calcium and magnesium content which would otherwise, over time, leave deposits in pipes.

Water supplying taps for drinking or cooking purposes come straight from the mains supply, other water will feed a storage tank such as for hot water installations. Such tanks constitute a serious health risk if they are not correctly covered, cleaned and maintained. In the past, they have been found to contain the bacteria associated with Legionnaire's disease.

Bacteria which cause this disease favour temperatures of 20–45°C and slow-moving water. Temperature control is therefore one precaution which can be taken.

Hot water is a legal requirement in most public buildings (see the Offices, Shops and Railway Premises Act 1963) and the temperature needs to be safe but effective and economic to produce and maintain. Estimated hot water requirements for hotels are 115–135 l per person per day and an average temperature is 55°C. The main methods of producing this hot water are:

- central storage plant and distributive pipework, servicing the whole building
- remote storage plant, heated from a common heat source, with zone distribution pipework
- local storage vessels, heated by independent sources
- local, instantaneous water heaters.

Factors to consider in the selection of an appropriate system include:

- adequate provision for peak demands
- economy of fuel, fuel storage, heating apparatus and installation
- distribution system, with minimum 'dead legs' (long lengths of pipes through which hot water must pass before emerging at taps)
- maintenance
- hot water storage
- capacity
- temperature requirements
- aesthetics of visible elements and reverberation of pipes.

Heating

Heat is both gained and lost by buildings as is shown in Table 3.3.

The actual requirements of heating systems will vary according to the room temperatures needed. In determining

Table 3.3 Heat transfer within buildings

Heat gains	Heat losses
Occupants (depending on age, activity, etc.)	Building materials (depending on 'U'* value)
Solar gains (depending on orientation, time, etc.)	Ventilation (depending on rate of air change)
Lighting (depending on source)	Building construction (depending on materials and degree of fit)
Electrical and mechanical equipment	Refrigeration plant (also a heat source)
The heating system	

*'U' value of building materials is the measure of the rate of thermal transmittance

temperatures, relative humidity (usually 30–60 per cent) should be considered as well as factors listed in Table 3.3. In most situations, the aim is for a 'comfort zone', where 85 per cent of users feel comfortable. The heating system will need to be flexible to meet changing needs and there are five main types:

1   warm air – heated air is fed into rooms via ducts
2   underfloor – heating grids are fitted in the floor screed (often using off-peak electricity)
3   ceiling – low temperature radiant elements are fitted between ceiling joists and the final finish
4   localized heaters – small moveable or fixed units
5   radiator systems – these are the most common and consist of:
    ● central boiler (gas, oil or solid fuel, some boilers being designed as high efficiency)
    ● distributive systems and pipework (including pumps, gravity, one or two pipe systems with the transfer medium being air, pressurised water or steam)

- emitters (e.g. pipes, radiators, convectors, skirting heaters and panels).

Energy conservation

Whichever heating system is used, it should be economical. Estimates in the UK show 30 per cent of total energy produced being used to heat buildings and around 3 per cent of hotel running costs being spent on energy. There may be considerable scope for the facility manager to make real savings here and some of the factors to consider are as follows.

- Insulation of heat sources, distributive systems, room spaces and buildings themselves.
- Avoiding over-heating, comfort being affected by the balance between temperature, humidity and velocity of air movements (draughts).
- Only heating areas to comfort conditions when they are to be used (e.g. some areas may not be used at weekends, others are unused at night). Time clocks, thermostats (possibly computer-controlled) and zoned heating systems may be appropriate.
- Distribution systems need to be designed to minimize 'dead legs'.
- Regular maintenance of all heating components to maintain maximum efficiency.
- Heat recovery and recycling (e.g. laundry processes generate considerable heat, much of which can be reused, and heat pumps may be used).
- Raising staff awareness with 'switch off' campaigns, etc. A rise 1°C above the desired level, can have a disproportionately large effect on overall energy consumption.

With competitive pricing being an important factor in many hotels, a saving of 1 per cent on energy costs could provide the chance for price reductions – giving a marketing advantage to the hotel.

Ventilation

The purpose of the ventilation system is to maintain oxygen supply and appropriate humidity, whilst removing carbon dioxide, excess moisture, odours and other gases. At the same time, comfortable air velocity is required. There needs to be a feeling of air movement, but usually air speeds should not be greater than 0.5 m/s. The temperature of the fresh air should not vary greatly from the room or mixing will not occur. In cold weather, fresh air may need humidifying. In warm weather, drying of air may be desirable.

Ventilation can be:

- natural, using windows and doors (where air movement is induced by temperature effects or wind)
- mechanical, where air movement is controlled by powered fans
- a mixture of the two.

As with heating, the occupiers of a space and the type of activity will determine the type of ventilation system required. Sports areas, for example, will require lower humidity levels to maintain comfort than office areas. In some areas, humidifiers are used to treat the water vapour content of air.

Besides maintaining the oxygen and humidity balance, air entering buildings or specific rooms may be filtered or cleaned by other means. Air conditioning plants control air temperature, humidity, gas content and purity. They are sometimes used as a means of controlling energy usage, for example heat need not be lost as stale air is removed – the warm air can be used to heat incoming, cooler air. Ionizers may also form part of the air conditioning plant or be fitted separately. These are designed to control the positive–negative ion balance of the atmosphere. High concentrations of negative ions are claimed to affect both mental and physical health.

Lighting

The lighting system of a building must meet a variety of needs, depending on particular users and their activities. For example, people in a reception area, staff carrying out office work, guests waiting for a lift and housekeeping staff cleaning a carpet will all have different lighting needs.

Some of the aspects to consider with respect to the lighting system are shown in Figure 3.3.

Within a building there is natural light and artificial light. In the interests of energy conservation, use may be made of available natural light – the amount and quality depending on orientation, cloud cover, time of day, environment, window and glazing type.

There are three main types of artificial light in building interiors:

1   tungsten, where fittings are cheap but inefficient in energy use and have relatively short lives

Figure 3.3 The components of a lighting system.

2   fluorescent, where fittings are more expensive, more
     efficient and last longer
3   new generation discharge, which are more expensive, more
     energy efficient and last longer.

Exterior lighting by artificial means, is usually achieved by
sodium discharge lamps, mercury halogen or tungsten halogen.

Information technology

In the past, buildings have been constructed, then cabling for
telephones and other electrical apparatus added. The enormous
impact of IT in recent years has demanded that this be
recognized as a standard, in-built service, in the same way that
heating, lighting and ventilation have been previously. Broad-
band networking within buildings and appropriate computer
and communication facilities can result in an integrated communication system, including telephone systems, data systems
and audio-visual services. With good planning at the design
phase, all these services may be incorporated into a common
cabling structure, but the key factor is to plan extra capacity,
particularly in terms of local terminations, for future increases
in demand. The technology to provide a common 'terminal'
to replace all controls, alarms and consumer appliances (e.g.
TV, video and telephone) along with substantial advances (e.g.
tele-video communications) is currently available, the only
question being cost (which is rapidly decreasing).

Some of the key features to be considered when planning
the IT facility for hotels are shown in Figure 3.4.

Sick building syndrome

The symptoms of sick building syndrome include irritation to
the eyes, nose, throat and skin, headaches, lethargy, irritability
and lack of concentration. These symptoms are more common

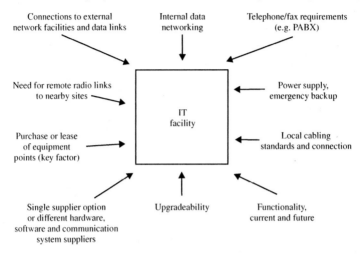

Figure 3.4 The components of an IT facility.

in the users of some buildings than others and most often, though not exclusively, described in office environments, particularly those which are air conditioned. The effects of sick building syndrome for businesses include reduced productivity, absenteeism and increased staff turnover. One estimate (Raw, 1993) is that 30–50 per cent of buildings are affected.

The causes and their combinations seem to vary, but it is thought that they include ventilation systems (particularly where these include a cooling system), temperature over 21°C, low humidity, subliminal flicker of fluorescent lights, indoor air pollutants (including dust) and volatile organic compounds from furnishings, adhesives, building materials, cosmetics, cleaning equipment and office materials. This is an area which requires more research, but it seems that the main issues for the facilities manager to address concern:

● the implementation of high standards of cleaning to maintain low levels of airborne dust (good filtration systems on suction cleaners and damp, rather than dry, dusting techniques)

- the planned maintenance of air conditioning and ventilation systems to ensure cleanliness
- the provision of good lighting.

Surface coverings

Selecting surface coverings (e.g. floors and walls) can only be effective when the characteristics of a material are matched with the specific needs of the area in question, bearing in mind installation, amount of use and availability for maintenance.

The fundamental properties of materials relate to:

- stiffness – the ability to recover, depending on stress (e.g. elasticity)
- strength – the force it can withstand before being broken
- toughness – the resistance to cracks.

These basic properties vary in any material, depending on its condition (e.g. whether under compression or tension) and the temperature (steel is strong, but at low temperatures, it is brittle).

Floor coverings

During the life of a building, about three-quarters of all cleaning costs will be spent on floor maintenance and statistics show that 16 per cent of accidents at work happen at floor level. Careful selection of the covering can ensure that the daily appearance is good, the floor is safe and the maintenance costs are minimized. Terotechnology involves the analysis of life-cycle costs of materials (i.e. cleaning and maintenance costs), as well as initial capital costs. In the case of floor coverings, this can result in considerable, long-term savings.

In preparing a performance specification for a floor covering, installation, replacement and repair need consideration, as does the compatibility of the floor surface with the type and condition of the sub-floor. Aspects to consider with respect to material properties are shown in Table 3.4.

Depending on their structure, floor coverings have been classified as:

- porous (e.g. wood, cork and concrete)
- semi-porous (e.g. vinyl, vinyl asbestos, PVC and thermoplastic)
- non-porous (e.g. epoxy resin, quarry tiles and marble)
- soft floor coverings.

The porosity of the floor will greatly influence its resistance to soilage and, therefore, the required maintenance. Depending on the maintenance programme, inherent properties such as attractive appearance, durability, chemical resistance, water resistance and slip resistance may be enhanced.

Wall and ceiling coverings

Wall coverings, although usually less vulnerable than floors, may still need to withstand a certain amount of abrasion, spillages and other moisture. Characteristics to consider in developing performance criteria for wall and ceiling coverings are shown in Table 3.5.

The range of wall and ceiling coverings is considerable, but the main categories are:

- paints
- papers
- plastic
- fabric (wall)
- other natural materials (e.g. timber, cork, stone, metal and glass).

Table 3.4 Material properties and their relevance to floor coverings

Material property	Possible application to floor coverings
Acoustic properties	May need to be sound reflecting or absorbing
Aesthetic value	Significant in prestige areas and appearance retention important
Colour and pattern	Variety may be important, also retention and effect on apparent soilage
Corrosion resistance	Consider spillages, sunlight degradation
Cost	Depends on replacement cycle
Durability	Depends on type and amount of use
Electrical resistance	Consider in areas where static electricity may develop
Elasticity	Consider quality of subfloor
Function	Consider maintenance
Light reflection	For aesthetic and safety reasons
Porosity	Consider spillages, type and maintenance
Prestige	Consider in relation to aesthetics
Resilience	Affects comfort of users
Slipperiness	Important – particularly the effect of moisture
Strength	Consider impacts (compression)
Temperature resistance	Consider cigarette burns and insulation
Transparency	Usually opaque required
Toughness	Resistance to abrasion, cutting and falling objects

Table 3.5 Material properties and their relevance to wall/ceiling coverings

Material property	Possible application to wall/ceiling coverings
Acoustic properties	May need to absorb radiating noise (e.g. in restaurant)
Aesthetic value	Appearance can dramatically change that of a room
Colour and pattern	Variety can be important
Corrosion resistance	Grease and condensation in kitchens
Cost	Depends on replacement cycle
Durability	Consider resistance to rubbing
Elasticity	May need to cover surface defects
Electrical resistance	Will contribute to overall static levels in room
Function	Consider use of area
Light reflection	Depends on colour, texture and gloss
Porosity	Acoustic and soilage resistance properties could conflict
Prestige	Consider visual appearance
Resilience	Impacts in busy corridors
Slipperiness	Less relevant
Strength	Consider impacts
Temperature resistance	Flammability could be important
Toughness	Consider abrasion resistance
Transparency	Usually opaque

Glazing

Glazing is taken to include external and internal windows and partitions, glass coverings and mirrors. As with any surface, the specific use will determine the criteria for selection. The main types are:

- soda lime glass, which includes toughened, laminated, tinted, patterned, wired and organic coated
- lead crystal
- borosilicate.

Several types of plastic are used in glazing instead of glass, the most common being:

- polymethyl-methacrylate (acrylic)
- polycarbonate
- polyvinylchloride (rigid PVC).

In glazing, plastics generally have a higher resistance to impact than glass does and are lighter. Glass has better clarity, fire resistance and chemical resistance.

Sanitary fittings

There are two types of sanitary fittings, namely soil appliances (used for collecting excretory matter) and waste appliances (for kitchen, washing, bathing and other waste). The materials used for sanitary fittings are:

- fireclay
- vitreous china
- cast iron
- vitreous enamel steel
- stainless steel
- plastics acrylic or glass fibre reinforced acrylic plastic.

In selecting sanitary appliances, material properties which need to be considered include weight and ease of installation, resistance to heavy use and occasional misuse, impact and scratch resistance, heat resistance and retention, slip resistance and chemical resistance. The auxiliary fittings (e.g. plugs and taps) must also be considered.

Water conservation can often be effectively managed by:

- the design and size of the fitting
- the flushing mechanism
- the taps fitted (e.g. spray taps)
- the plug and ease of use.

The minimum numbers of fittings required in public buildings is specified under the Health and Safety at Work Act 1964, and depends on the use of an establishment and the number of users.

Furniture

Generally, furniture needs to be functional, it is needed to enable an activity to occur, or to occur with greater comfort. The basic criteria for functionality are shown in Figure 3.5. If furniture is comfortable to use, it is less likely to be misused and 'live costs' will be reduced.

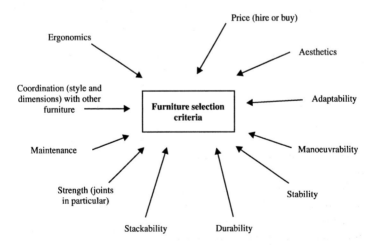

Figure 3.5 Furniture selection criteria.

Textiles

Textiles surfaces, like wall coverings, are likely to have relatively short lives. By replacing furnishings fairly frequently, the overall style of the establishment can be changed to meet changing demands. Textiles include carpets, upholstery, cushions, pillows, towels, uniforms, bedding and bed linen and curtains.

Fibres are classified as natural (e.g. wool, cotton, linen and silk) and manufactured, including regenerated fibres (e.g. rayon) and synthetic (e.g. polyamides and polyesters). The type of fibre influences the characteristics of the finished product including its strength, elasticity, thermal, chemical and electrical properties and the effect of sunlight and moisture. From the fibre, the yarn itself can impart different characteristics on the fabric (e.g. mixing fibres of different colours or types or texturing of synthetic fibres to form crimp, bulk or loops).

Fabric is produced by weaving, knitting, felting or bonding and these processes too will significantly affect the characteristics of the finished fabric. For example, pattern can be produced, textures varied, elasticity, strength and thermal properties all affected. The finished fabric may then receive further treatment (e.g. dyeing, printing, fire resistance processing). In selecting fabrics, therefore, the required characteristics should be carefully considered to enable an informed choice of fabric and finish to be made.

Interior design

To achieve optimum conditions for customers and staff, the design of the building structure, environmental services, surface fittings and furnishings must all be integrated, to produce functional surroundings providing the right ambience and atmosphere. The overall appearance of an establishment is an essential part of merchandising and product image. The integration of the key design elements is shown in Figure 3.6.

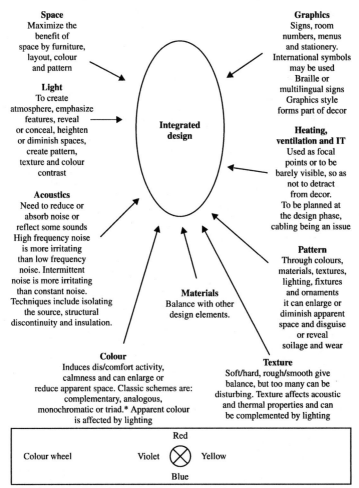

Space
Maximize the
benefit of
space by furniture,
layout, colour
and pattern

Light
To create
atmosphere, emphasize
features, reveal
or conceal, heighten
or diminish spaces,
create pattern,
texture and colour
contrast

Acoustics
Need to reduce or
absorb noise or
reflect some sounds
High frequency noise
is more irritating
than low frequency
noise. Intermittent
noise is more irritating
than constant noise.
Techniques include isolating
the source, structural
discontinuity and insulation.

Colour
Induces dis/comfort activity,
calmness and can enlarge or
reduce apparent space. Classic schemes are:
complementary, analogous,
monochromatic or triad.* Apparent colour
is affected by lighting

**Integrated
design**

Graphics
Signs, room
numbers, menus
and stationery.
International symbols
may be used
Braille or
multilingual signs
Graphics style
forms part of decor

**Heating,
ventilation and IT**
Used as focal
points or to be
barely visible, so as
not to detract
from decor.
To be planned at
the design phase,
cabling being an issue

Pattern
Through colours,
materials, textures,
lighting, fixtures
and ornaments
it can enlarge or
diminish apparent
space and disguise
or reveal
soilage and wear

Materials
Balance with other
design elements.

Texture
Soft/hard, rough/smooth give
balance, but too many can be
disturbing. Texture affects acoustic
and thermal properties and can
be complemented by lighting

	Red	
Colour wheel	Violet ⊗ Yellow	
	Blue	

*Complementary colour scheme is one where colours are chosen from opposite sides of the colour wheel.
Analogous colour scheme where adjoining colours on the colour wheel are used
Monochromatic colour scheme where only one colour is used with various tints and shades
Triad colour schemes use contrasting colours on a neutral background

Figure 3.6 The elements of an integrated design.

Principles of design

In Figure 3.6, a constant interlinking and cross-referencing of design elements can be seen. Elements cannot be considered independently. Lighting installations affect colour perception, accentuate pattern and texture and can enlarge or diminish apparent space.

Colours must be balanced with pattern and texture and selections made in the lighting conditions of that space. Acoustic properties are affected by texture, material selection, dimensions of space and situation. In this way, elements intermingle and, to achieve good integration, the following overall principles have been identified.

- Unity, variety and balance should be achieved in line, form, texture and colour. If several colours are used, texture and pattern variations should balance this. A sense of order is required, without becoming monotonous.
- One centre of interest or one dominant idea should be identified.
- The design should incorporate rhythm, which is a means of leading the eye to the centre of interest.
- There should be good proportions and scale of patterns, furniture and dimensions.

Integrated design must create environments which are, above all, safe to use. They must be practical and they must achieve the right atmosphere for the planned activities.

Housekeeping and maintenance

Having considered the design and construction of the hotel and the fittings, furniture and furnishings, it is appropriate to review the processes whereby these important assets are maintained. 'Housekeeping' relates to the cleaning and care of the interior of a building and the provision of certain tangible client services. 'Maintenance' refers to the upkeep of the fabric of the building, including the exterior and site, the plant, equipment and services. In both cases, to be effective, the functions need to be planned. As part of the facilities management remit, the functions should not operate on a reactive, *ad hoc* basis. Instead, they should be delivered on a scheduled basis, with the flexibility (as with other services) to meet changing needs.

Planned cleaning and maintenance

Planning the cleaning and maintenance programmes is more beneficial than a purely reactive approach in the following ways.

- **Financial benefits** Costs are balanced out over a cycle, rather than a large number of replacements or expensive servicing being needed at the same time. Costs can be forecast and provision made in the budgets to cover them. Regular cleaning and maintenance will delay deterioration of many items, thus making direct savings on budgets.
- **Functional benefits** The downtime (of equipment or areas), is planned to occur at the most convenient time and the probability of breakdowns or other failures is reduced, as servicing is planned to occur before normal failure. In this way, accidents too may be reduced.
- **Aesthetic benefits** The appearance of surfaces is maintained. Appearance and apparent cleanliness have a psychological effect on building users, customers and staff alike, affecting feelings of well-being, the reputation of the hotel and repeat business.
- **Human benefits** Clean, attractive, well-maintained surroundings encourage high working standards, pride in work and personal appearance and increased staff morale. In addition, the Health and Safety at Work Act 1974 does require a duty of care with respect to all building users.

Preventative maintenance

Well-planned cleaning and maintenance programmes will also be preventative maintenance programmes. Plant, equipment and surfaces can be kept in such a state that failures and breakdowns are minimized. To achieve this, failures and normal deterioration must be anticipated and procedures for prevention devised. Risk analysis can assist in this. By this process, all possibilities are identified, consequences quantified and probability of occurrence measured. The programme of cleaning and maintenance based on this prioritizes on the basis of risk and effects.

A planned preventative maintenance programme must:

- ensure that legal requirements are met
- meet operational needs
- have the commitment of senior management
- be cost effective (i.e. the costs of planning and monitoring must not outweigh the savings derived).

However, some breakdowns (even disasters) can be predicted only by the use of remote statistical data and predicting the timing of occurrence is impossible. Certain preventative measures may practically be put in place, but the law of diminishing returns applies. The probability of the event occurring is so small and the measures to be taken to further reduce the possibility of the event occurring so costly, that it is only practical to plan a disaster recovery process. This is a process of identifying possible reactions which will alleviate the difficulty as soon as possible so that the inevitable disruption to business is minimized.

The scope of maintenance

This is shown in Table 3.6.

A building survey will need to be undertaken to evaluate

Table 3.6 The scope of maintenance

Building elements	Internal	External
Plant	Heating, lighting, ventilation, lifts, escalators	Lighting, fuel sources
Services	Electricity, gas, water, waste collection, telecommunications and cabling	Drainage, external infra-structure
Machinery and equipment	Catering, laundry, cleaning, fire-fighting, access, electrical apparatus	Transport, access, fire-fighting, waste disposal
Building envelope	Doors, windows, walls, ceiling, paintwork, structural repairs, redecoration	Roof, guttering, fire escapes, masonry, paintwork, windows, structural repairs, redecoration
Site		Gardens, pathways, fences, gates, boundaries, walls, car parks, barbecue areas

and record each building element, service, utility, plant and piece of equipment. It will list relevant details of construction, materials or serial number, age, state, maintenance details and expected life. This database will form part of the hotel's total asset register. By keeping such data over a period of time, a cost pattern for each building element or item can be developed enabling maintenance schedules to be determined.

Preventative maintenance, relating to larger and less frequent activities, involving high expenditure, can be planned, as can some procedures which will occur on a frequent and regular basis. However, it is not possible to plan all maintenance in this way. The maintenance system must also be able to react to unexpected breakdowns and requests from other building users. Such work tends to involve a high proportion of small, urgent jobs. Generally, maintenance tasks are scheduled on a short-term (or even immediate), medium-term or long-term basis. Computer-based project management techniques can be used effectively to plan these medium- and long-term activities, in such a way as to make the most efficient use of resources.

Control of the maintenance programme

In planning long-term maintenance activities, some tasks will be scheduled to occur on a regular basis (e.g. servicing of equipment.) Whatever system is used, whether manual or computerized, it should readily identify when such tasks are due. There will also be a need to ensure effective use of staff and equipment, and record costs.

Often a system of job costing can be useful, whereby cost (including materials, parts and labour) is estimated and then adjusted in the light of experience. This becomes the standard cost and is valuable in analysing the percentage expenditure on activities such as painting and decorating. These records can be used to analyse trends, forecast future expenditure and to inform decisions regarding outsourcing or contracting out.

Alternatively, in other costing regimes, maintenance costs can be expressed in terms of cost per $100 \, \text{m}^2$, aggregated and compared with initial building cost or analysed by cause (perhaps as part of a post occupancy survey of a new building). Analysis of such factors as those resulting from property design, construction materials, technical errors, layout, changes in user expectations or changes in use might be recorded. In

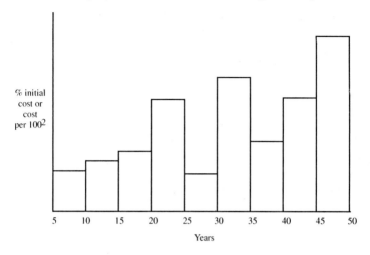

Figure 3.7 Example of an hotel maintenance profile.

the standard system of hotel accounting, the one item which needs to be measured and costed separately is that of energy.

The pattern of maintenance costs over the life of a building is known as the 'maintenance profile' and a sample is shown in Figure 3.7. Such profiles can be used as the basis for benchmarking, comparing one hotel with another.

Another document of value in the management of a building is a maintenance manual. This contains working, up-to-date plans of the building, dimensions of each area, specifications of materials, maintenance requirements and treatments given. Passed from one owner to the next when the property is sold, this can be invaluable to subsequent facilities managers.

The scope of the housekeeping department

Housekeeping services largely relate to the cleaning of the building interior and may or may not include cleaning of linens and soft furnishings. In addition, service elements also form part of the remit of this department, such services might include provision of early morning teas, luggage packing and unpacking, child minding, personal laundry service and bed turning down.

The aim of cleaning is to remove as much dirt as possible and, where possible prevent or reduce re-deposition. Generally, standards of cleanliness are defined as either 'aesthetic' or 'clinical'. Aesthetic standards aim to achieve a clean, pleasant and attractive appearance, whereas clinical standards aim to remove as much soilage and, thereby, micro-organisms as possible, prevent cross-infection and provide a specified standard of hygiene. The type of cleanliness and the standard will depend on:

● the users' requirements
● the users' activities (e.g. eating a meal or using the games room)
● the infection risk, as in kitchens or sanitary areas
● the type of establishment – whereas the hygiene standards in a small guest house would need to meet the same as those in a luxury hotel, appearance standards (e.g. shine on a floor surface) may be lower.

Finance also plays its part – the more frequent the cleaning, the more expensive the programme.

Hygiene

Surveys conducted in hotels to ascertain guest requirements frequently show that, above all, customers want *clean* accommodation. Public buildings, by their nature, provide sources of infection and victims for infection – individual guests might be carrying an infection or be particularly susceptible to infection. The infection cycle comprises a source, a link and a potential victim, as shown in Figure 3.8.

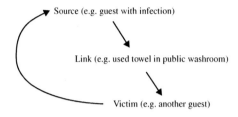

Figure 3.8 The infection cycle.

The aim of cleaning is to break the link in the cycle. In the example in Figure 3.8 this could be achieved by the provision of paper towels or possibly a hot-air hand dryer. Other examples of 'links' might be poorly laundered bed linen, uncleaned glasses in ensuite bathrooms and uncleaned crockery. Once infection has been deposited on surfaces to thrive, warmth, moisture and a nutrient source (e.g. dirt, which inside buildings frequently contains dead skin scales) are required. A few bacteria can very quickly multiply to become large colonies. Conversely, to kill bacteria, the only really reliable method is heat treatment, which is appropriate for laundry work and dish washing, but not a feasible treatment for surfaces such as floors and furniture surfaces. Here, thorough cleaning (i.e. removing soilage) must be relied on. This can remove up to 85 per cent of micro-organisms and, to achieve this, cleaning equipment must be effective at loosening and gathering the soilage. In this way, an ordinary neutral detergent will help to break up grease and allow the soilage to be released.

Although chemical disinfectants of various types are available, dilution rates are critical. Some surfaces can inactivate them, as can bad storage. The duration of the contact between the chemical and the infection can be important, as can the temperature. Altogether, effective cleaning is more reliable than dependence on chemical disinfectants alone.

Other sources of infection could include vermin or insects, which are frequently attracted to the warmth and food sources provided by public buildings. Another source could be cleaning equipment itself. If this has been used and put away dirty, bacteria will have bred and, when next used, the equipment spreads infection instead of reducing it. Cleaning of equipment should be part of all hygiene procedures.

In providing a cleaning programme which breaks the link in the infection cycle, it must be remembered that the person executing the cleaning process must also be protected from infection. This can be achieved largely by good personal hygiene, particularly washing hands, but protective clothing (e.g. overalls and rubber gloves) are also generally required. Precautions against infection by the HIV virus include:

- disposal of sharp items (e.g. razor blades) in impenetrable containers, rather than ordinary waste bins
- the use of a safe disposal system for sanitary towels and nappies
- high standards of laundering and safe handling of soiled linen
- towels not being used by more than one person
- the use of rubber gloves when cleaning blood, vomit or excreta, and the hygienic disposal of mopping materials and laundering of contaminated clothing
- the use of hypochlorite disinfectant – effective if used correctly.

The control of housekeeping

The necessity for a planned approach to cleaning and maintenance has already been argued. With respect to cleaning, this will involve analysis of what needs to be cleaned, how it should be done, how often, by whom and when. As with maintenance, a building survey will need to be conducted to produce an inventory for each area. In the case of housekeeping, the asset register will be used to identify items for cleaning, their size and their surface material.

Figure 3.9 shows a room schedule format which could be used to gather the relevant information. The 'comment' column could include details of furniture density, periods of use, frequency of use, general standards required and condition of the fabric. All these factors would affect the cleaning programme. This schedule could be further developed by adding a column for 'task' (e.g. shampoo, suction clean, damp dust and early morning teas) and possibly another for

Establishment		Room name/code	C32
Gables Hotel		**Location**	C block
Room Type			
Guest room			
Dimensions			
4 x 5 m			

Item	Quantity/dimension	Description	Comments
Floor	20 m²	80/20 Wilton	Entrance area showing wear
Chairs	2	Draylon upholstered	Light beige
Stool	1	Draylon upholstered	Light beige
Divan bed	Standard double	Pine bed head Sprung mattress	Bed head is wall mounted

Comments

Figure 3.9 A sample room schedule.

the frequency of each task (e.g. shampooing annually and suction cleaning daily).

Once all room schedules have been produced, including analysis of tasks and frequencies, the tasks can all be collated in a standard procedures document. This will detail the cleaning procedure for each task. The actual process will affect the time which needs to be allotted and the supplies needed and with standardization of procedures, training packages can be developed which meet the needs.

Pest control

All service operations have an obligation under the Prevention of Damage by Pests Act 1949 to protect the health of the public and prevent loss and damage to property by pests. Not only can pests carry infection, they can also cause considerable damage to property and be visually offensive. Reputation can suffer if pests are sighted by customers or infestations made public.

Table 3.7 outlines the main groups and types of pest, together with the harm associated with them.

Good pest control involves identifying potential risks and then discouraging infestation by preventing access to buildings or by ensuring dry, clean surfaces which will not support the organisms. Spillages need to be cleaned effectively and waste managed efficiently. Where infestations do occur, it may be necessary for these to be irradicated, through chemical or other means.

Security

In the design of a building, great care and consideration must be given to the aspects of security. Systems may be developed to improve security by developing staff awareness and controlling building access. However, security cannot be considered

Table 3.7 Pest types and associated harm caused

Group	Types	Associated harm caused
Insects	Bed bugs, fleas, ants, flies, cockroaches, silverfish, moths, mites, woodworm, death-watch beetle	Carrying bacterial infection, damage to materials and fabric, skin irritation and reaction, visual offence
Rodents	Rats, mice	Carrying infection, damage to materials and fabric, visual offence
Birds	Starlings, pigeons, gulls	Fouling carries infection, causes damage and is offensive
Fungi	Wet rot, dry rot	Damage to wood structures and furniture

as an 'add on', it must be built in to the design of a new building. Public buildings are inevitably security risks, by the very fact that so many people have access to them. They must, therefore, be designed and constructed for security, without this conflicting with welcoming the *bona fide* customer.

Security provision must be made for the protection of all building users, buildings, interior plant, equipment, furniture and furnishings and for property owned by staff and customers. Security threats include intrusions, attack, vandalism, dishonesty and fire.

The siting of entrances and the internal layout can greatly assist in the monitoring of those entering and leaving the building. Lobbies, entrances and waiting areas are particularly able, as they are public places. It is necessary, at the planning stage, to identify the potential security risks in order to take the measures needed to minimize them. These may include surveillance equipment, security lighting, locks and other systems to control access (e.g. intercom systems, key systems, alarms, high security spaces, safety deposits and tagging devices).

A safe working environment

In planning and designing an hotel, the focus of attention is on the customer. The benefits of a customer-focused approach have already been discussed. However, the facilities manager has responsibilities for all building users and other stakeholders in the enterprise and by providing good working conditions for staff, efficiency, productivity and motivation levels will be enhanced.

Probably the most hazardous area in an hotel is the kitchen. Some of the hazards here include:

- the overall temperature and humidity
- slip hazards through spillages
- burns and scalds from cooking activities
- electrical appliances
- moving appliances
- cuts
- lifting heavy items (i.e. pans and sacks of ingredients)
- bending for low ovens, etc.
- chemicals for dishwashing and cleaning
- fires.

In housekeeping and laundry work, hazards relate to:

- chemicals
- scalds
- lifting heavy items and climbing step ladders

- bending (e.g. bed making)
- electrical appliances
- dealing with soiled items
- noise
- slipping on wet floors
- airborne dust
- cuts and infection from dealing with waste.

Maintenance and grounds work hazards include:

- electrical appliances
- lifting and climbing
- cuts and infection from waste
- fumes from chemicals, paint and seals
- injuries from tools
- dealing with waste.

Reception and front office work hazards might include:

- the implications of using visual display units for long periods
- the implications of key boarding for long periods
- stress caused by peak demand periods of customers checking in and out.

Portering hazards obviously include lifting.

These hazards need to be identified and addressed by the facilities manager in terms of removing or minimizing the risk. A real commitment to a safe working environment and the application of some lateral thinking may well enable safer working conditions to be achieved. In some cases, there may be a conflict between the needs of the staff and those of guests. For example, temperature requirements for those working in a restaurant will be lower than for those sitting and eating a meal and there may be only a limited amount that can be done about finding a compromise temperature. The hotel will not want to drive customers away from the restaurant because they are too cold, but in selecting uniforms for restaurant staff, the room temperature will need to be considered.

If hazards cannot be removed, how can the risk of injury be reduced? Solutions include using equipment designed with safe use in mind, training staff to work safely, to spot and deal with hazards, providing protective clothing and machine guards, designing safe systems of work and ensuring a planned preventative maintenance system is applied. Inevitably, when dealing with potential hazards, there will be some financial implications and a decision has to be reached as to whether to spend money preventing one potential accident or another. The process of risk assessment involves not just hazard spotting, but subsequently estimating the probability of the accident happening and were it to happen, what the consequences might be. In this way, resources can be targeted where they will have greatest benefit and an action plan produced to demonstrate the overall picture of the approach to achieving a safe working environment.

Finally, the aim of the hotel should be zero accidents, but if one should occur there needs to be a system, the expertise and the equipment for dealing with it. First aid facilities are a legal requirement, as is the recording and reporting of accidents at work.

The Health and Safety at Work Act 1974 has far-reaching implications for any work situation, ranging from the overall duty of care of all employers and employees, to the very specific requirements of the Care of Substances Hazardous to Health Regulations (1994) and the Safety of Electrical Equipment Regulations (1989). The emphasis is on prevention and the facilities manager will of course need to be well informed about such legal aspects. The overall working environment may be causing unnecessary pressures. The facilities manager should also consider the application of ergonomic theory and method study techniques (see Chapter 5).

The building then is a major resource for any hotel and if maximum benefit is to be derived from it, all aspects – from design through to maintenance – must be managed effectively.

References and further reading

Jones, C. (1997) *Facilities Management in Hotels*. PhD thesis, Derby.

Brand, S. (1994) *How Buildings Learn: What Happens After They're Built*. Viking, Penguin.

Raw, G.J. *et al.* (1996) *A Questionnaire for Studies of Sick Building Syndrome*. Proceedings of the CIBSE National Conference, 1996. Watford: Building Research Establishment.

Lawson, F. (1981) *Conference Convention and Exhibition Facilities*. Architectural Press Ltd.

Worthing, D. (1995) *Strategic Property Management Facilities Management Handbook* (A. Spedding, ed.).

4
The provision and specification of facilities services

Aims and objectives

This chapter aims to:

- identify alternative means of service provision and consider the application of contracting out and outsourcing in the hotel context
- differentiate between contracting out and outsourcing
- emphasize the importance of continually reviewing existing service provision
- emphasize the need to understand the true cost of the existing provision and to carefully analyse the true cost of any contracting out or outsourcing intention
- consider criteria on which to base contracting out and outsourcing decisions, including their advantages and disadvantages
- describe service specifications and service level agreements
- outline the tendering process, including the process for small contracts and the relevance of the Transfer of Undertakings (Protection of Employment) Regulations (1981).

Provision of facilities services

The range of facilities services to be provided and their significance to the core business will be variable. They may be managed in an integrated way, grouped under one manager, or they may be managed in a fragmented way as separate services. All the services may be provided by in-house teams of staff or all or part of the services may be provided by external suppliers. Even where facilities services are provided totally by external suppliers, it is necessary to have an in-house manager responsible for coordinating the provision and liaising with the external providers, who has ultimate responsibility to the customer for the provision of the service.

Companies are increasingly considering outsourcing as a strategic option. Since the early 1980s, following a precedent set by the Ministry of Defence, Government policy has dictated that public sector organizations (e.g. the National Health Service) and then local authorities undertake compulsory competitive tendering. The philosophy behind this dictate is to market test the cost effectiveness of private sector suppliers against in-house provision in order to discover whether savings can be made and resources redirected to the core business of the organization. Over the last 20 years, the emergence of the philosophy of compulsory competitive tendering together with the unprecedented rate and range of change enforced on organizations, such as rightsizing and flattening structures, has created the need to constantly refocus on competitiveness and operational efficiency particularly of the core business. This, in turn, as explored in Chapter 1, has led to organizations increasingly considering the options of contracting out or outsourcing some or all of their facilities management activities. This has stimulated an increase in the number and range of facilities services and suppliers.

It is unusual in an hotel context to totally contract out or outsource the whole facilities services provision. In most hotels, it is common to provide most of the services in-house with the possible exception of:

- linen and laundry services, which involve large capital investments in linens and equipment and require a discrete area of operation

- periodic cleaning and maintenance tasks (e.g carpet shampooing or sanding of wooden floors), which require specialist knowledge and/or equipment
- activities such as window cleaning and sanitary and waste disposal, which are hazardous or unpleasant activities, and which are repeated on an on-going basis
- daily cleaning of all public areas
- pest control services.

However, situations do exist where property owners or asset management companies retain control of the property but contract out or outsource the whole hotel management function (including facilities management).

Is there a difference between contracting out and outsourcing?

There is a difference, although the terms tend to be used interchangeably. It is useful to adopt Barrett's (1995) distinction. Barrett describes contracting out as the process by which a user organization employs an external supplier organization, under contract, to perform a function (e.g. window cleaning or carpet shampooing), which could alternatively have been performed by in-house personnel if they or the equipment were available. Outsourcing, according to Barrett, is the process by which the user organization employs an external supplier organization to perform a function which has previously been undertaken in-house and which involves not only the transfer of assets (e.g. people and machinery) but also management responsibility to that supplier. Contracting out is more relevant for hotels.

Evaluating current service provision

In today's threatening and rapidly changing climate, organizations, – public and private and large and small – need to continually re-evaluate their business objectives and strategies in order to survive, remain competitive and grow. This will involve critically evaluating current service provision, determining the extent to which it fulfils customer expectations, targeting areas for change and redefining the service which is required now and into the future.

The following fundamental questions need to be asked.

- How are facilities services organized elsewhere?
- Is existing provision and service delivery efficient and cost effective?
- How do provision and service delivery rate in comparison to other sources of supply?
- Are the facilities services customer-oriented and do they satisfy customer expectations?
- Can the quality of services required for the next five years continue to be delivered?

Feedback from internal and external customers will provide an invaluable source of information. In the case of the maintenance and cleaning service, fulfilment of the needs of the physical asset will also need to be re-evaluated by means of a building appraisal. Other evaluative techniques may include:

- SWOT analysis to determine the strengths, weaknesses, opportunities and threats in the various elements of the service or function
- value analysis to consider the impact on costs and profitability of potential changes to processes, procedures, resources and purchasing decisions.

This appraisal may lead to the need to consider contracting out or outsourcing options. The decision to provide an in-house service or to totally or partially contract out or outsource is very complex and it may be appropriate to appoint a project manager and establish a core team of key service operations managers to undertake the initial evaluation, make the appropriate decisions for change and manage any subsequent transition. The impact of any potential change on the whole organization, its structure, processes and personnel must be very carefully considered. In conjunction with this, the organization's core business may need to be re-examined, the advantages and disadvantages of each strategic option balanced, the negative and positive effects of outsourcing existing provision considered and the criteria on which to base the contracting out or outsourcing decision determined.

Analysis of true activity costs

This is relevant on two levels. First, it is essential to know the true costs of existing service provision. Analysing the true costs of the services may be difficult, hampered by the cost structure of the organization and difficulties associated with allocating overheads to specific activities or functions. Such an analysis involves identifying those costs associated with pre-production and/or service delivery, actual and post production and/or service delivery. This analysis provides the opportunity to reduce or eliminate all unnecessary or non-value-added costs and consider future value-added costs. It is important that organizations try to understand the true activity cost and determine the true marginal cost before embarking on an outsourcing exercise. One appropriate evaluative approach is value chain analysis. This is a process which isolates the core activities of an organization so that their costs and the differences between alternative means of provision, now and in the future, can be better understood (Rothery and Robertson, 1995). Ways of undertaking these activities more cheaply or better than the organization's competitors can be sought in order to gain a competitive advantage. This approach enables likely outsourcing components to be identified. It highlights the relationship of these strategically relevant activities to other components of the organization and their role and, thus, identifies whether they can be classified as strategic components or a competitive advantage.

Often service providers within an organization are traditionally organized as cost centres and service costs are not charged back to the user of the service. An alternative strategy to outsourcing may be to convert service cost centres to profit centres in order to stimulate competition and to enable the service provider to buy and sell on the open market. This introduces market forces and eliminates captive business. This can empower the service provider to generate income and alleviate excess capacity and downtime problems during periods of low demand. For example, where an on-site laundry is unviable but has spare capacity, an alternative option to outsourcing is to sell laundry services to other organizations in the vicinity and, thus, generate income.

Second, an exhaustive and accurate cost analysis should be undertaken before entering into any outsourcing agreement. Many organizations underestimate the costs involved and their cost justification for the outsourcing decision is frequently inaccurate (Chalos, 1995). Outsourcing, particularly total outsourcing, 'is only worth the effort if there is a sizeable saving' (Sharpe, 1993: 28). There is evidence to suggest that outsourcing can increase rather than decrease costs (Chalos, 1995). The cost analysis includes production and/or provision costs, transaction costs and coordination costs.

Transaction costs include costs involved in searching for reliable suppliers, administering the tender process and evaluating, entering into and enforcing contracts. This includes the time spent by staff, project coordinator, senior management and any consultants employed. Coordination costs include all costs associated with the changeover from in-house provision to outsourced supply, plus coordination and monitoring over the entire life of the contract. These costs may include:

- switchover of software licences
- penalties for premature termination of leases
- severance pay

- retraining of in-house staff to coordinate and interface with the terms of the contract and the outsourcing staff
- the appointment or retention of a technical expert to monitor the contract over its duration.

Other costs which are difficult to project and which may lead to higher costs than anticipated relate to potential breach of proprietary information, the financial stability of the supplier, unexpected demand and unwillingness of the supplier to invest in new technologies. The summation of all these costs can rival the economies realized in production and service costs. So what initially appeared to be an appealing outsourcing option may under close scrutiny prove unattractive.

Another danger is that outsourcing decisions are often based on short-term cost and cash-flow considerations, as when a company has an immediate liquidity problem, rather than longer-term strategic planning. This is partly because user demand patterns and cost and technology projections are so difficult to predict. Short-termism can lead to poor outsourcing decision making.

More effective outsourcing decisions will be made if the organization is thoroughly familiar with the market and prevailing conditions. In an outsourcing situation, the organization may be at a severe disadvantage if it does not retain a knowledge of on-going changes in the market place in order to keep in touch with what is happening and, thus, does not retain bargaining power. It is also essential, when a contract has been let, to install the necessary systems to monitor and measure resultant changes in output, throughput, activity and marginal costs and to prevent any savings being passed onto the outsource supplier. Organizations may enter a partnership arrangement with the supplier to share such savings.

Re-examining core business

When re-examining core business, it is necessary to identify the core competencies on which the organization's ongoing success and survival is based and to consider what impact the outsourcing decision will have on them. The core competencies may be human resource related and include a particular set of staff or a group of skills or they may be technological in nature and related to equipment, processes or the physical building. How core these competencies are will be a matter of judgement, influenced by the structure of the organization and how it functions. A particular service may be deemed to be core, but some parts of it and some staff may not actually be so.

Criteria on which to base the contracting out or outsourcing decision

These criteria must be explicit. A hotel would not wish to contract out or outsource any activity which is too critical to the success of its core business (e.g. the management of room sales or quality management). Any activity which provides a unique competitive advantage (e.g. unique skills or competencies), high value-added processes or cutting-edge technology may put the organization at risk if outsourced. Generally, an hotel would not contract out or outsource a core service which can maintain a steady workload or where only one external supplier is available.

Based on Hodgson's (1996) suggestions, contracting out or outsourcing may not be an option where:

- it is beneficial to the organization to retain in-house provision
- the total cost of purchasing including transaction costs (see page 103) is more than that of undertaking it in-house
- it would have a major impact on employee relations or overall staff morale
- the organization does not have the capacity to monitor and manage the contract.

On the other hand, contracting out or outsourcing might be an option (Rothery and Robertson, 1995) where activities:

- are very labour intensive
- fluctuate with considerable peaks and troughs
- are commonplace and not unique to the organization
- need high capital investment in equipment and plant
- require discrete areas of operation (e.g. an on-site laundry)
- are specialist and/or support activities
- are subject to quickly changing markets where staff need to be retrained or new staff recruited and trained
- require expensive and rapidly changing technology.

Balancing the advantages and disadvantages of in-house and contracting out or outsourcing options

There are many reasons why organizations consider contracting out or outsourcing. The most frequently cited are the alleged economies of scale and specialist skills which can be passed on by specialist suppliers who are providers to many purchasers. In theory, such economies should lead to cost savings which at best could be shared by both partners but at worst cede to the supplier. Other perceived advantages are listed in Table 4.1.

There are also perceived disadvantages of contracting out or outsourcing. These are given in Table 4.2.

A useful exercise in the decision-making process is to compare the advantages and disadvantages of resourcing in-house provision against the advantages and disadvantages of contracting out and/or outsourcing (Barrett, 1995).

Outsourcing is not a cure all or quick fix solution to a long-term problem (Sinensky and Wasch, 1992), nor is it the right solution for every business. Many organizations do not realize the benefits that they anticipated (Chalos, 1995). However, outsourcing is a potentially beneficial strategy when used in

Table 4.1 Perceived advantages of contracting out and outsourcing

---

Can increase productivity and operational efficiency
Concentrates on core business
Releases management talent and money for real strategic business concerns
Uses available capital to invest in core rather than non-core business
May yield cost savings through reduction in labour costs or administrative workloads
Eliminates staff availability, recruitment, sickness and labour turnover and staff travel problems
Reduces management responsibility for labour and eliminates responsibility for industrial disputes
Causes a rethink and respecification of service requirements
Improves or guarantees levels of service
Enhances customer service
Injects competition and realism
Eliminates problematic, time-consuming, difficult, hazardous or monotonous tasks
Provides specialist skills and equipment not available in-house
Releases capital and avoids further investment for new or replacement equipment
applicable for a new unit
Fixes the budget
is a way to access state-of-the-art technology and training
Reduces accommodation and space needs or costs (e.g. by relocating IT to a lower cost geographic area or into a larger centralized site maintained by the outsource supplier)
Provides specialist expertise on an as needed basis
Increases flexibility if permanent workforce is reduced
Client and supplier can work together, building loyalty to mutual advantage

---

(Adapted from Barrett, 1995)

Table 4.2 Perceived disadvantages of contracting out and outsourcing

---

Claimed savings not always realized
Personnel problems created with regard to change-over and transfer of assets
Lack of control over suppliers
Risk of selecting poor supplier who cannot fulfill conditions of contract or is insufficiently competent
Insufficient suppliers to cope with demand
Lack of loyalty to organization and its users
Insufficient understanding of the organization's core business
Contrary values and ethics
Confidentiality of data
Security risks
Exchange one set of management problems for another
Retain need to coordinate and monitor
Risk of contracting out critical aspects of business
Loss of in-house expertise, capability and market knowledge
Lack of flexibility through long-term fixed contracts
Supplier's capacity, availability, accessibility and lack of commitment
Continuity of staff
Hidden costs
Time involved in tendering and setting up contract
Learning curve of supplier may be slow
Slower response time to problems
Reliance on one supplier

(Adapted from Barrett, 1995)

the right circumstances, by the right companies (Sinensky and Wasch, 1992), if specialist skills and economies of scale do truly exist, if contracts are enforceable and if the strategic mission of the organization is not impaired.

The negative and positive effects of outsourcing

If the outsourcing exercise is not managed effectively, it can have a negative effect on staff morale. Employees are understandably anxious and uncertain about the future. The process can take months of negotiations and rumours can run rife. Employees may feel unwanted by the organization, productivity can decrease and many staff, particularly the best ones, begin to look for other jobs. Key people resign and valuable experience and company 'memory' is then lost (Due, 1992).

An organization could select a provider who is unable to deliver what has been promised or it could negotiate a poor contract which leads to loss of service quality. The economies of scale offered by the supplier may mean in fact that it is unable to respond quickly to new technology or developments and the purchasing organization may lose the ability to evaluate new technology. A lack of new ideas could permeate throughout the organization and lead to mediocrity. Indeed, the purchasing organization may become a hostage to the outsource supplier, locked into a unique relationship, and suffer from the management and financial problems of the supplier. Start up costs, lack of expertise and lack of an in-house workforce place the organization in a weak bargaining position.

On the positive side, outsourcing may provide new training and promotion opportunities for staff who remain in the organization and staff who are transferred. There could be the challenge of a new work style and possible enhanced perks and company benefits.

Specifying the service

Whatever the outcome of the evaluation process, it is essential to define the service and its components which are to be provided, either in-house or externally, in order to satisfy the needs of the customers. There are two slightly different approaches to achieving this. The first option is to develop a service specification, which is usually the case in a contracting out or outsourcing situation. The second option is to produce a service level agreement, which is more usual for the in-house provider to produce in conjunction with internal customers.

The service specification

The purpose of the service specification is to set out the requirements for a particular service operation. The service specification normally contains:

- a definition of the service required
- the quality of service expected
- the framework for monitoring service delivery (see page 199)
- penalties for non-compliance
- issues to be reviewed during the life-cycle of the contract (e.g. the review of a particular part of the service).

By way of an example, the service specification for the cleaning or housekeeping service would specify:

- the physical areas of the property to be included within the provision by means of a schedule of accommodation
- the tasks, activities or services to be performed
- definitions of all technical terminology
- relevant policies on the Care of Substances Hazardous to Health Regulations, sharps, infection control and the use of chemical disinfectants
- explicit standards of quality to be achieved (see page 200)
- how the process will be monitored and controlled (see Chapter 7).

The service specification then forms the basis of the tender specification or in the case of in-house provision a service level agreement (see below) against which the tenderer (in-house provider or external contractor) submits a delivery specification (see page 160).

The service specification must be complete and unambiguous to minimize the risk of misinterpretation and omission. This is particularly so in the case of contracting out or outsourcing, as any activities omitted will not be undertaken by contract staff and will result in negotiating 'alterations' to the contract which will involve further costs. There is a danger of over specifying requirements, thus encroaching on the service delivery domain, constraining operational practices and increasing costs. A balance between over specification and generalization has to be found. In the case of a cleaning specification, expected frequencies of tasks are not always specified. This allows the tenderer or provider to determine the optimum frequencies to be undertaken to achieve the minimum acceptable standards stated. This then provides a point for comparison between tenderers in a competitive situation.

The service specification provides the basis for estimating staffing and supervisory levels, formulation of deployment and coverage plans, and, thus, budget formulation.

Service level agreements

The first such agreements developed for in-house service providers were pioneered by computing services. Contracts with external service providers may include service level agreements. In fact, Hiles (1993) suggests that often external contracts are vague and service level agreements can be used to supplement them. A service level agreement may also be known as a 'customer supplier agreement'.

Hodgson (1996: 232) defines a service level agreement as 'an agreement between the provider of a service and a user of that service quantifying the minimum acceptable level of quantity and quality to be provided'. Hiles (1993: 2) suggests that in practical terms this means that 'if you do this, then I will do that and this will be the cost'. In reality, a service level agreement is virtually a combination of the service or tender specification and the service delivery specification (see page 160) forming the basis of an internal agreement.

The nature of the internal provision situation is rather different as the service level agreement is grounded in a joint exploration of what is in the best business interests of the internal customer. Thus, the degree of collaboration between the provider and the internal consumer is much greater than in an external contracting situation and the latter asserts more influence on the nature of the service provided. A service level agreement contributes to achieving greater efficiency in the use of an organization's resources and is particularly useful where conflict exists between provider and consumer – particularly in the case of fluctuating demand. For example, where a service provider cannot control fluctuations in demand, a service level agreement can be used to create an internal trading system whereby provision of the service is dependent on income from the user. The agreement should contain ground rules limiting the user to using only the in-house service. The customer needs to supply accurate utilization and volume forecasts and must agree to meet agreed deadlines and targets with regard to consistent volumes of work and not exceed a defined peak demand limit.

Quantifying service is a vital element, particularly in terms of monitoring and measuring performance. As stated in the definition, the service specification should be based on the minimum service level acceptable to meeting the customer's requirements. This will involve exploring various service level scenarios and identifying the level which can be cost justified. Over-providing quality obviously is more expensive.

The minimum level of service also has to be explored. Hiles (1993) suggests that there are four levels of service from non- or self-support by the customer to a low, a medium and a high level of service. Over-specification of the level does not necessarily translate as a better service – just a more costly one. The range of services to be included also requires definition. The service level agreement should identify service parameters in terms of identifying service products, availability (taking into account critical times), performance (in terms of speed, job turnround, response times and accuracy), process performance measures and control, security criteria, points of delivery and delivery mechanisms. Such a service level agreement is particularly apt between the front of house operation and maintenance when planning an extensive refurbishment programme.

Although the basic principles of a contract apply in so far as an offer is made to provide a service on specified conditions and an agreement to this constitutes an acceptance of the offer, a service level agreement as an internal contract is not legally enforceable. Nevertheless, the service level agreement should be adhered to with both parties signing the agreement and keeping copies. The process of arbitrating disputes must be clearly stated. Price and pricing variations to the service level agreement must be clearly understood and be realistic in terms of available budgets.

Service level agreements promote a customer orientation within the service operation and emphasize the supplier customer chain which is internal to the organization. Internal customers are supported in the achievement of a business or commercial orientation, with the process fostering the evolution of a service culture.

Procuring external facilities services

The complexity of the contracting out or outsourcing decision will depend on the scope and size of the potential contract. At one end of the continuum, a manager could be considering a single one-off contract which for some reason has not or cannot be undertaken in-house. Such contracts might include the periodic cleaning tasks or maintenance activities referred to earlier which the in-house team are not capable of undertaking without further training or which would not be possible without the purchase of new capital equipment. Such a small single contract may involve only a few hours of work. On the other hand, the window cleaning or waste disposal contracts also referred to earlier, which involve an activity repeated on an on-going basis and which are contracted out because they are hazardous or unpleasant occupations requiring specialist equipment and expertise, constitute larger single contracts.

At the other end of the spectrum, an organization may be considering total outsourcing of all non-core activities, including facilities services and administration services (e.g. health and pension benefits and payroll processing, personnel management, training and development, accounting and auditing) and occupational health services. In this case, the decision is further complicated by the need to consider the advantages and appropriateness of the 'one cheque' or single sourcing approach where the whole contract is let to one supplier. The alternative approach to this involves letting a series of smaller or sub-contracts to a number of companies. This is a more efficient way of diversifying risk, but is more time consuming to administer. Large contracts tend to be for a three-, five- or ten-year duration particularly when it is necessary to transfer some or all of an organization's existing plant, systems and operation's personnel. Contracts tend to be shorter where there is uncertainty about future developments (e.g. with regard to IT and other technological developments).

There are cases where total outsourcing has led to a new independent entity being established to take ownership of the transferred assets. Existing employees are terminated and reemployed by the new company and new employment conditions are negotiated. (See the Transfer of Undertakings (Protection of Employment) Regulations (1981) page 123).

The tendering process

Procuring facilities services, particularly from external suppliers, involves a process known as the tendering process which can be broken down into four definable stages – a pre-tender stage, the tender stage, the evaluation and the appointment. Each stage is further subdivided in Table 4.3. In the situation where

Table 4.3 The tendering process

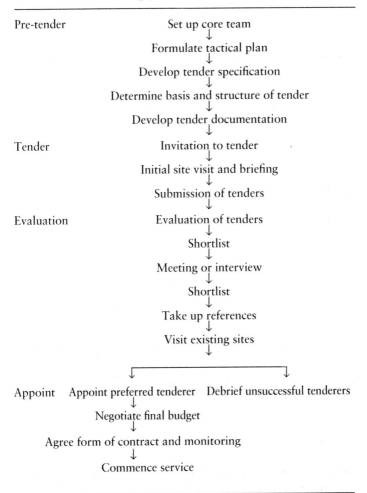

Pre-tender	Set up core team
	↓
	Formulate tactical plan
	↓
	Develop tender specification
	↓
	Determine basis and structure of tender
	↓
	Develop tender documentation
	↓
Tender	Invitation to tender
	↓
	Initial site visit and briefing
	↓
	Submission of tenders
	↓
Evaluation	Evaluation of tenders
	↓
	Shortlist
	↓
	Meeting or interview
	↓
	Shortlist
	↓
	Take up references
	↓
	Visit existing sites
	↓
Appoint	Appoint preferred tenderer Debrief unsuccessful tenderers
	↓
	Negotiate final budget
	↓
	Agree form of contract and monitoring
	↓
	Commence service

in-house provision is being market tested, the in-house provider would be expected to tender in competition with external contractors or outsource suppliers and follow the same tendering process. A similar, albeit simplified, process will be followed when a small one-off contract is to be let (see page 123).

The pre-tender stage

Core team

Outsourcing is a complex, time consuming and costly business and should not be treated lightly. If the contracting out or outsourcing exercise is to stand any chance of success it requires total commitment at executive level and the support of a high level corporate framework incorporating the necessary resources. Where an organization is continually reviewing its current service provision then no doubt a project coordinator and a core team of appropriate key service operations managers will already exist. If not, this core team needs to be established with a project manager to coordinate the whole tender process.

Tactical plan

A comprehensive plan, detailing intentions, purpose, outcomes, management responsibilities, timetables, deadlines, resources and budgets, will facilitate the exercise. Where appropriate, the role of the trade unions and their involvement in the process must be decided at this stage.

As with any new initiative, final outcomes depend on the initial vision. All stakeholders must share a common understanding of the purpose and reasons for change and the anticipated aims, objectives and outcomes to be realized. Therefore, all these aspects must be clearly identified and defined at the outset. Relevant company policies and codes of practice may need revision and dissemination.

Service or tender specification

The service specification (see page 110) provides the basis of the tender specification, which provides the necessary framework and details against which the tenderer (in-house provider or external contractor) submits a delivery specification. It also provides a tool for the comparison of tenders at the evaluation stage later in the tendering process.

Basis and structure of tender

Guidelines on how to tender and the form of the tender to be submitted need to be drawn up. The latter, plus the provision of standard forms for specifying key information, greatly facilitate evaluation of tenders and decision making.

Tender documentation

The tender documentation normally incorporates the conditions of tender, that is what to tender for, how to tender, the form of the tender to be submitted, the terms and conditions of the contract (see Table 4.4, and the service specification (including policy documents).

The tender stage

Invitation to tender

A list of potential companies to be invited to tender will have to be established. This will involve deciding whether to adopt a selective tendering or open tendering approach. Selective tendering involves drawing up a shortlist of desirable companies to invite to tender, whereas open tendering involves advertising to allow any company that wants to to tender.

Table 4.4 Terms and conditions of a contract

Goods and services to be provided
Standards of quality required
Price to be charged
Circumstances under which prices can be changed
How payments are to be made
How invoices will be validated
The facilities to be provided by the organization
Warranties, indemnities and insurances to be evidenced
How disputes will be resolved
Penalties for non-performance and non-conformance
Duration of the contract
Default and termination arrangements
How contractual variations, i.e. deletions and inclusions will be
agreed and charged
Ownership of supplies
Control of assets
Management cover
Security arrangements
How emergencies will be dealt with

Selective tendering is often preferable as the number of tenderers are limited to a practicable level. Selective tendering involves identifying and appraising potential suppliers. This, in turn, involves scrutinizing company and financial reports and even visiting the companies in order to evaluate their technical and managerial capacities. Tenderers will then be issued with the appropriate documentation as specified earlier.

Initial site visit and briefing

All potential tenderers, including the in-house provider if it proposes to tender, should be invited to visit the organization. This provides the opportunity to survey the premises, plant and equipment, perceive existing standards and ask questions. To ensure fair play and consistency, the site visit should be conducted by the same person or team preferably on the same day.

Submission of tenders

Potential tenderers will then produce and submit their tender in conformance with the specification and according to the specified procedure and deadline. The tender submissions will be based on the principles involved in developing a service delivery specification as discussed in Chapter 5.

The evaluation stage

Evaluation and comparison of tenders

This can be helped greatly by clearly stating in the tender documentation the form of tender to be submitted and by providing standard forms for highlighting key details. An example of such a standard form used for comparing key financial details of cleaning tenders is given in Table 4.5.

Evaluation should be undertaken by a panel of experts and should not include any representative of the in-house service involved in the preparation of the in-house tender (if there is one). It may be appropriate to consult with the trade unions at this stage.

Evaluation of tenders involves assessing the overall competency of the supplier to deliver the service or function specified and fulfil the conditions of the contract. This is often referred to as vendor rating or supplier performance rating. It involves evaluating some or all of the following performance dimensions:

- price
- quality
- delivery
- commercial viability

Table 4.5 Checklist for evaluating key financial details
of cleaning tenders

Name of tenderer
Tendered price per annum
Tendered price per week
Worked hours per week
Notional cost per worked hour (i.e. tendered price per week
divided by worked hours per week)
Supervisory hours per week
Supervisory ratio (i.e. worked hours per week divided by
supervisory hours per week)
Management hours per week
Cleaning equipment and materials cost per annum
Cleaning equipment and materials as a percentage of the
tendered price per annum (i.e. cleaning equipment and
materials cost per annum as a percentage of tendered price
per annum)
Allowances for absence, holidays and sickness
Basic pay rate per hour
London weighting

(Department of Health, 1989. Crown copyright is
reproduced with the permission of the Controller of Her
Majesty's Stationery Office.)

- technology
- management capability and cover.

For example, in addition to the checklist in Table 4.5, performance rating of cleaning tenders might include consideration
of:

- hours worked
- rosters
- shift patterns
- employment levels and patterns

- annual leave entitlements and sickness allowances
- equipment and materials provision
- training
- quality control/assurance
- staff workwear and personnel identification
- costs of covering unscheduled work
- references
- company accounts
- relevant company policies.

Where possible, evaluation should be based on quantitative ratings to overcome the deficiencies of subjective rating (including the 'halo' effect, which is the tendency to be biased in favour of a supplier by some quite irrelevant impression or estimate – good or bad – of that supplier) (Lysons, 1986). Quantitative rating of the performance dimensions could involve allocating a priority rating value to each dimension according to its importance, then scoring each dimension on, say, a one to ten scale and calculating the total score for each potential supplier.

On completion of this analysis, it is useful to record the cost of each tender in ascending order on a summary sheet and to ask the following questions.

- Does the submission meet the specification?
- Are there any omissions?
- What is the cost in the first period and over the duration of the contract?
- How does it compare with the other tenders?
- Has the supplier got the capability to fulfil this contract now and in the longer term?
- Are the standards and values of the potential supplier consistent with the organization?
- Is any further information required?
- Do any points need clarification?

Shortlisting and interviewing

The purpose of evaluation is to determine which suppliers can be rejected and which can be invited for interview. Ideally, a short list should comprise two or three companies to be invited for interview. This interview should be conducted by the same panel involved in the evaluation of the tenders and provide equality of opportunity to all shortlisted tenderers. The interview enables both parties to ask further questions and seek clarification. The panel may then be able to eliminate one or more of the tenderers.

References and site visits

At this stage, the organization will need to take up references and may well visit other sites where the tenderers already provide the same or similar service and/or their head office. The purpose of the visit must be carefully considered, but it is basically to observe and question existing clients and users. Dimensions to be considered might include:

- the attitudes of staff towards their work and the degree of interest they show in customer service
- quality of staff output
- the atmosphere of harmony or dissatisfaction amongst staff
- adequacy and care of equipment
- technological know-how of team leaders
- method of controlling quality
- general housekeeping arrangements, in terms of cleanliness and orderliness
- the competence of staff and management.

A final decision can then be made. Cost alone should not dominate the outcome.

The appointment stage

The preferred tenderer will be appointed and a meeting convened to negotiate the final budget price, to agree improvements in performance and to confirm the form of contract delivery. Debriefing of unsuccessful tenderers is an extremely important activity at this stage in order to maintain goodwill and reputation. The evaluation process should enable feedback to be given on how performance could have been improved.

Further meetings will be arranged with the appointed contract supplier to make the necessary arrangements for handover and transfer of any assets. Involvement of key personnel and training of relevant staff will facilitate a smooth changeover.

Strategic alliances

It may be appropriate to consider developing a strategic alliance (Chalos, 1995) with the potential service supplier. A synergy may be created by collaborating with an outsourcing partner to effect economies of scale, risk diversification, increased market potential and innovation. Strategic alliances are often essential to international competitiveness. They can be formed with both suppliers and customers to diversify into new areas of activity or even forestall new players into the market place.

The letting of small contracts

This will involve following the same tendering process, albeit a simplified version (as detailed in Table 4.6). Again, someone within the organization will have to be designated to coordinate this activity.

It may be necessary to have a formal interview as well as a site visit. The basis and structure of the tender will not be as complicated nor the documentation as comprehensive.

Table 4.6 Process involved when letting a small contract

Consult with key personnel
Prioritize the activity
Consider its purpose
Identify applicable company policies
Decide whether the activity really should be contracted out
Formulate a tactical plan
Evaluate how and when this activity will fit into the current service
Analyse the cost of the activity and other cost implications
Prepare a specification of exactly what needs to be done
Provide the necessary documentation to the selected suppliers
Select potential suppliers/providers, invite them for a site visit and briefing
Evaluate and compare prices
Take up references
Undertake the vendor rating process
Appoint a supplier to undertake the contract

The Transfer of Undertakings (Protection of Employment) Regulations (TUPE) 1981

These Regulations are designed to protect staff terms and conditions in transfer. They are an enactment of the EC Acquired Rights Directive 1977, which lays down broad guidelines intended to safeguard employment rights for staff transferring under arrangements like compulsory competitive tendering. The Regulations stipulate that when a supplier undertakes work previously undertaken in-house, staff who previously did the work have the right to transfer to the new organization on no less favourable conditions of employment. In the early days of compulsory competitive tendering, private sector suppliers were able to undercut internal tenders through cutting pay rates and eliminating other costly employment benefits such as double time for Sunday working. Contractors now have to compete by making services more effective rather than just cutting rates of pay (Hodgson, 1996).

The problem is in determining when the Regulations apply and whether outsourcing is a transfer of undertakings. Barrett (1995) suggests that clarifying the answers to the questions listed below should help in determining whether or not the Regulations apply, but that this still only points towards the Regulations applying.

- What is the type of service or function? Define it.
- Are tangible assets, such as buildings and plant, to be transferred?
- Are intangible assets, such as trade names and intellectual property rights, to be transferred?
- Are the majority of the services employees being transferred to the potential supplier?
- Are the service's customers being transferred?
- Will the function of the transferred service be recognizably the same after transfer?
- Will the transfer include previously let contracts made between the user and other contractors?
- Are trade debts being transferred?
- Are restrictive covenants being transferred?

References and further reading

Barrett, P. (ed.) (1995) *Facilities Management: Towards Best Practice*. Blackwell Science Ltd.

Chalos, P. (1995) Costing, control and strategic analysis. In *Outsourcing Decisions in Cost Management*, 31–7.

Department of Health (1989) *Format for the Structured Presentation of Domestic Services Information*.

Due, T. (1992) The Real Costs of Outsourcing. In *Information Systems Management*, Winter 1992, 78–81.

Hiles, A. (1993) *Service Level Agreements – Managing Costs and Quality in Service Relationships.* Chapman and Hall.

Hodgson, K. (ed.) (1996) *Managing Health Service Contracts.* WB Saunders Company Ltd.

Rothery, B. and Roberston, I. (1995) *The Truth About Outsourcing.* Gower Publishing Ltd.

Sinensky, A. and Wasch, R.S. (1992) Understanding outsourcing: a strategy for insurance companies. *Journal of Systems Management*, January, 32–6.

Sharpe, R. (1993) Boom or bust? *Computer Weekly*, November 25, 28–30.

5

Designing the facilities services operation delivery system

Aims and objectives

This chapter aims to:

- identify the remit of a service operation and the primary responsibilities of the service operations manager
- describe the transformation process central to converting key input resources into primary and secondary outputs
- identify the components of a facilities services delivery system and explore factors which affect its design
- briefly consider a secondary output of the transformation process, namely waste and its disposal.

The service operations remit

Operations management provides the means by which an organization implements its strategic plan, achieves its objectives and delivers to its customers. The main responsibility of the service operation is, therefore, to achieve the organization's objectives through the delivery of the service as defined in a contract specification or a service level agreement or by the executive and, thus, meet the needs of its customers (internal and external). The service operations manager must understand the strategic plan and share the same vision of the organization as the executive. The operations might need to ask the same strategic questions as the organization has asked at a higher level.

- What are our strengths, weaknesses, opportunities and threats?
- What are the values and aspirations of all major stakeholders, including customers and managers?
- What are our social responsibilities and objectives (Henley Distance Learning Ltd, 1991)?

Operations management is, therefore, primarily concerned with the following.

- Meeting customers' needs – failure to do so enables another provider to grasp the opportunity and meet their needs more effectively.
- The efficient management of resources, including:
    - staff
    - physical assets
    - systems
    - finance
    - equipment
    - materials and commodities.

In an hotel context, the physical assets, which constitute the core business, and the staff who contribute to the provision of the core business and the satisfaction of the customers, are *the* key resources. In reality, resources are rarely adequate and the operational management challenge is to acquire and exploit resources with maximum efficiency whilst meeting the customer needs as effectively as possible.

- Improving performance and productivity whilst achieving low operating costs. In today's environment, operations managers are pressured into developing products and services and achieving continuous improvements in performance and practice to gain competitive edge whilst making increasingly greater efficiency gains.

The transformation process

At the heart of any operation is a process which converts inputs or resources (e.g. equipment, people, skills and competencies) into outputs (e.g. goods, products or services) for the customer. This is fundamentally a change or transformational process which is described in Figure 5.1.

In reality, service operations comprise a whole series of smaller, but interrelated, input and output activities each of which transforms designated inputs into defined outputs in a structured and controlled manner by means of procedures and standards. Customers' needs contribute to the definition of the desired outputs.

Components of a service delivery system

These will be the same whether delivery is made by an in-house facilities service operation or outsourced to a

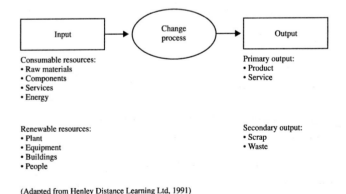

(Adapted from Henley Distance Learning Ltd, 1991)

Figure 5.1 The transformation process.

facilities management contractor. In either case, it will be necessary to consider the following.

- What is the nature of the markets to be served?
- In what manner will the defined markets need to be served?
- What is it that the service operation has to deliver?
- What is the nature of the products and services to be provided?
- What are the outputs to be achieved?
- How can these defined outputs best be achieved?
- What could prevent the outputs being achieved?
- When and where do these outputs have to be achieved?
- What key input resources are needed to make it happen?
- How can these key input resources be managed efficiently?

The delivery specification provides the infra-structure to enable the service package as defined in the service specification or service level agreement to be supplied – to both internal and external customers – within a number of parameters, particularly cost and time. Efficiency of delivery is centred on understanding how the components of the delivery system interact and the processes involved work, the capabilities of the delivery mechanism (i.e. the people and the equipment), the importance of achieving consistency of performance of both production and service operations, and the tolerances within which they can operate. The components of the delivery system are outlined in Figure 5.2.

Interpreting the service specification and defining service provision

In many organizations, the facilities services have to be provided or supplied within the constraints of a service specification or service level agreement. Such specifications (as discussed in Chapter 4) define:

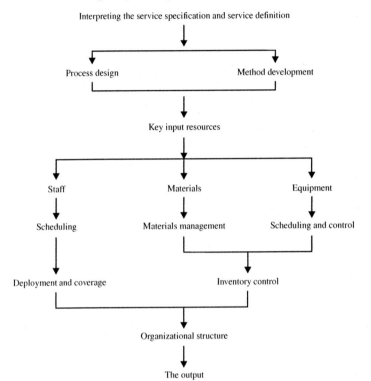

Figure 5.2 The delivery system.

- the types, range and level of service(s) required
- such service parameters as availability, response times, security arrangements and meeting set quality levels and performance standards
- reporting and liaison arrangements
- customer responsibilities
- cost constraints.

In the absence of a specification or where existing specifications are vague, an enlightened facilities services operations manager will clarify the terms of reference and boundaries of responsibilty. This is of particular importance where provision of facilities services is fragmented with discrete divisions responsible for separate facilities functions. For example, it may be unclear in an hotel operation whether food and beverage or housekeeping staff are responsible for particular cleaning tasks in the banqueting rooms, restaurants and bar areas or whether housekeeping or maintenance services are responsible for periodic floor maintenance activities.

Subsequently, the budgets of each facilities service must reflect the specific responsibilities of that service in order to enable effective financial control. It is difficult for the housekeeping division to monitor and control the cleaning materials budget, for example, if cleaning materials used by food and beverage staff are costed against the housekeeping budget.

Service definition will include clarifying:

- the types and range of services to be provided (see Chapter 1)
- the scope and boundaries of each type of service to be provided
- the points of delivery, location of activity or physical areas to be included in the service
- the tasks, activities, processes and operations to be included
- the frequencies of the tasks, activities, processes and operations and the availability of provision
- the quality standards to be achieved (see Chapter 7).

In a contracting situation, both the delivery and the quality assurance and monitoring systems will have been detailed in the tender submission document on which the decision to let a contract to a particular company will have been based. The provider then has to implement and manage the agreed service.

Process design

This involves understanding the nature and characteristics of the service operation, its location, process structure, alternative operating modes, work flow design and customer interface.

The nature of the process structure

Process structure is initially influenced by the type of output – whether tangible product or intangible service. Where the manufacture of tangible products is concerned, production is normally separated from consumption and decisions based on whether to:

- keep required input resources in stock in anticipation of production
- produce the product in advance and hold it in stock in anticipation of future demand
- produce as required and deliver without storing
- wait until specific orders are received and then acquire stocks and produce a customized product to order as in the just in time approach (see page 155).

In service operations, where production and consumption are 'on line' and take place in the presence or with the concurrent involvement of the customer, the necessary resources or product may be held in stock in anticipation of need or acquired as and when needed. The customer interface assumes an important impact on the process structure. In some operations, customers will be taken directly into the delivery system. In other operations customers will be expected to wait or queue (see page 139). For example, in a fast food outlet resources, the food product may be held in anticipation of customer arrival and then served immediately or within a few minutes of arrival. In other service situations, such as an à la carte restaurant it will not be possible to anticipate customer requirements and demand in advance, so customers will have to wait or queue whilst the resources are assembled in order to carry out the required production and service. In other service operations, customers might be required to queue even though the required resources are already assembled and product produced in readiness before arrival for instance boarding a plane or waiting entry to a conference dinner.

Appropriate mode of operation

This depends on the relative continuity of the operation. There are five definable modes of operation which are as follows.

1 The one off product managed on a project basis to meet the specific requirements of the customer. This would be applicable for off-site catering for a special event or function. Project management involves coordinating a range of varied activities and resources scheduled to achieve the customers desired results.
2 The 'jobbing' approach involves the provision of one off or small quantities which involve highly specialized processes customized to the user's requirements. This approach can be seen in, for example, cake decorating or in the maintenance context for responding to customer requests, like the need for extra shelves in an office.
3 Batch processing a range of products or services usually involves using the same facilities. Here the work pattern is repetitive within any individual batch but each batch may vary considerably. Batch processing normally enables faster processing. It happens in the laundry, where batches of sheets, towels, blankets or uniforms may be washed, hydro extracted and tumbled as discrete loads. It may happen in the front office, where manual posting of vouchers on to customer bills may occur on a batch basis rather than one here and one there as they arrive from the various sales

outlets. It may also happen as regards maintenance for cleaning light shades and changing light bulbs.

4 Line processing occurs where there is a high degree of repetition in the work pattern. Specialized equipment is often designed and deployed for a specific line and must, thus, be used intensively to justify the capital investment (e.g. in a bakery for different bread and confectionery lines). However, equipment and plant which is dedicated in this way often has limited flexibility and it may only be able to operate at a fixed rate of output.

5 Continuous production is very similar to line processing, but involves bulky commodities (e.g. cement or dirty laundry), rather than large numbers of smaller discrete items. Large modern laundries now use continuous tunnel washing machines where washing, rinsing, hydraulic hydro extracting occur at different places along the length of the machine and different loads are constantly fed in to the washer.

Work design and location of operation

Work design is influenced by the type and nature of the operation, particularly whether it involves production or service activities, the location of delivery and/or provision and the design and layout of the production and/or service areas. So catering will have allocated locations of provision and customers will travel to the service point. Processing of laundry will involve the flow of dirty linen from various areas throughout the building to a dedicated central site and distribution back to the points of usage. Catering and on-site laundry provision are manufacturing in nature, involving production processes and both require capital investment in specialized equipment and, therefore, a specially designed and discrete location. Good design and planning of the venue is an essential feature of these services as poor layout can increase processing time and create delays. Environmental conditions can also affect productivity and staff morale. Heating, lighting and ventilation systems must be appropriate to the nature of the service or product to be delivered and the activities to be undertaken. The ability to control and adjust them is of great importance.

The cleaning and housekeeping function is different in that it occurs throughout the building with staff travelling to an allocated area to undertake the service. In some cases, teams (e.g. floor teams) will be peripatetic – working their way around the building as scheduled. The building is usually divided into sections and sub-sections of convenient size to be tackled by an individual or group of staff, thus the majority of cleaning and housekeeping staff are isolated and work with the minimum of supervision. Self-motivation and self-discipline are key characteristics of a person specification in this context.

In maintenance, much of the work is based on jobbing or project management processes requiring detailed planning and the development of effective teams.

When designing the process system, consideration must also be given to:

- access to the service delivery point by suppliers, staff and potential customers
- availability of the service in terms of opening hours/times of operation to coincide with demand
- product distribution channels to points of delivery/ provision
- travelling time of staff to get to the point of provision
- security arrangements.

The work system consists of the interaction of staff, equipment and materials. The movement of these elements must be carefully planned. This can be achieved through the use of computer-aided design and, manually, through the use flow and string diagrams, operator process and multiple activity charts, and other work study techniques.

Good organization is required to keep the work flowing and increase productivity by limiting delays and transportation time or costs between elements of the system (Axler, 1976). The objective is to limit the processing time at each stage and the time between stages and prevent unnecessary movement making the flow of work as easy as possible. It will be more efficient to keep work flow moving in one direction, preferably in a short straight line, with each operation in a process next to the one before without backtracking, criss-crossing or changing directions. Guest room servicing is one example where this practice could make considerable savings. An efficient system of cleaning will not only reduce time but also ensure that standards of quality are maintained.

In an existing operation, ratio delay, which is a form of activity sampling, can be a useful technique to deploy. It involves observing staff, equipment and work at random and at regular intervals to study the relative activity of individual staff and equipment. The process identifies productive time and time which is used up by delays. The ratio of the delay time to total working time can be calculated and the reasons for delays analysed.

Delays include waiting for supplies or a piece of equipment, waiting for the completion of another operation by a different employee or waiting to gain access to an area. Ratio delay also reveals other unproductive time, such as collecting supplies, preparing for work, walking from one place to another and putting cleaning equipment away after use. This can occur in a large hotel where these delays could constitute as much as one to one-and-a-half hours within a room assistant's eight-hour shift. This can be translated into financial terms to realize the enormity of the problem. Planning work to reduce such under-utilized time is another means of improving productivity.

Network analysis techniques (e.g. critical path analysis) can assist in the scheduling of work activities. Network analysis involves identifying the sequence of tasks, highlighting which tasks are dependent on others, which are independent and which can be completed in parallel to others. The 'critical path', which is the sequence of tasks taking the longest time, can then be determined. In this way, waiting time can be reduced, labour costs minimized and the shortest completion time established. This approach is particularly applicable to project management such as a re-decoration programme.

Workstations need to be as self-sustaining as possible with all supplies required in close proximity to the point of operator usage. The siting of utility points (e.g. water points), utility rooms, cleaners cupboards, equipment and materials stores and service lifts will all impact on efficiency and productivity. Flexibility is a key feature of work design in terms of being able to change layouts and configurations if necessary and possibly use mobile work units if appropriate. The impact of mechanization and computerized control mechanisms will also need consideration.

The impact of the customer on service delivery

Customer contact stages

Six stages within the customer contact experience can be identified and are outlined in Table 5.1.

This concept is a more detailed variation of the guest cycle concept (Kasavana and Brooks, 1995) as an effective way for management to better monitor, chart and control guests' transactions. Plotting the sequence of the customers' activities by using a flow chart is a useful way of anticipating customers' needs and expectations at each stage in the contact cycle and, thus, determining appropriate organizational responses (particularly ways of managing customer movement and resource utilization).

Table 5.1 Customer contact stages

Stages	Description
Stage 1	Search – the customer is looking for a solution to fulfil his or her needs and contemplating using the product or service supplied by the organization/operation
Stage 2	Arrival – the customer makes the initial physical contact with the organization (this may include check in)
Stage 3	Pre contact – the customer awaits service and may have to queue
Stage 4	Contact – the customer receives the service and really engages with the organization
Stage 5	Withdrawal or departure – the customer leaves
Stage 6	Follow up stage – addressing remaining needs, gathering feedback, invoicing or promoting further services and events

(Adapted from Whittle and Foster, 1991)

Customer queues

In service operations, the need to manage customer queues may be of more significance than managing equipment and materials. Queues have been described as 'customers in storage', although queue management is an active process. In a service operation, customers are an essential input resource to all on-line activities. The function of a queue is to act as a buffer between the rate at which customers present themselves to the system and the rate at which they can be processed by it (Henley Distance Learning Ltd, 1991). Clearly, queues happen if customers arrive at the service point at a greater rate than the contact staff can accommodate them. If this difference persists, the queue grows longer and longer.

The facilities manager has to balance customer service and

deployment of resources and, subsequently, customer satisfaction against efficient use of resources. There is a need to keep resources fully occupied when there is no customer waiting, but under-resourcing can result in the formation of long queues and, consequently, customer impatience and the possibility of them transferring custom elsewhere perhaps on a permanent basis.

Customer queue management involves adjusting the number of service points to match customer demand and keeping queues to an acceptable length, particularly when it is difficult to predict customer flow.

The basic customer queue and service point configurations are:

- single line and single service point
- parallel lines and several service points
- single line and several service points.

The problem with the second configuration is that variations in the actual time taken to serve a customer will occur and, therefore, some queues will move faster than others. Some customers will change line in anticipation of quicker service. This may lead to anxiety and frustration particularly when customers are in a rush (e.g. when checking out of the hotel). It is essential to know the duration of the average transaction and to monitor and record demand and usage patterns.

Method and procedures development

Reliance on individual staff to interpret how to perform particular tasks, activities, services and produce products can lead to all sorts of problems, including lack of consistency and cost effectiveness and hygiene and safety risks. For consistency to be maintained, all staff must follow a standard method or procedure, based on best practice, of undertaking each task or activity. An example of a standard method would be cleaning the toilet. Standard methods may be referred to as job breakdowns, work procedures or job procedures. In the catering context, standard recipes are also included in this concept.

On the other hand, a standard procedure can be interpreted as an assembly of tasks required to complete a defined activity or service. They are often used in the housekeeping context to specify the tasks, the frequencies and time elements required to clean a particular room type (e.g. a bathroom or lounge). Standard methods and procedures contribute to setting standards of quality and are often coded for control purposes.

The development of a standard method involves the application of such work study techniques as method study, method improvement and motion economy. The method defined will influence the time required to perform the task. Whether an individual task or a series of tasks comprising a procedure for undertaking an activity or service, a 'task' analysis can be undertaken. Task analysis involves:

- isolating the task and defining it to avoid misunderstanding and misinterpretation
- identifying the objectives and purpose of the task
- developing the method of performance:
  - specifying the resources required in terms of equipment, agents, supplies and commodities
  - sequencing the stages involved in a logical order
  - highlighting hygiene, safety, security or any other key issues
  - describing the anticipated outcome or end result which will most probably be the 'minimum' or 'acceptable' standard to be achieved.

The benefits of this approach include:

- establishing the most appropriate method based on best practice
- providing a basis for training and monitoring

- specifying a standard for quality in terms of process and output (see Chapter 7)
- establishing a basis for uniformity and consistency
- standardizing on supplies and raw materials to effect economy of purchase.

The application of motion economy involves designing work and working methods which allow employees to perform tasks in the shortest possible time with the greatest ease and satisfaction, expending as little energy as possible. In conjunction with this, training of staff in the correct ways of lifting and handling in order to reduce fatigue and the risk of injury is important.

A standard operating manual or standards of performance manual, containing all the standard methods of performance or operating procedures, is useful for monitoring and control purposes and for inspection by such regulatory and inspection bodies as health and safety and ISO 9000 inspectors.

Frequency of activities

Frequencies, standards and costs are interlinked. A higher frequency of performance will result in a longer time allocation over a period, which results in higher costs. This may result in the achievement of a higher standard, but in some cases may actually lower the standard (e.g. if polish is applied too frequently the standard of appearance would diminish and further expense would be required to rectify the result). The challenge is to determine the optimum frequency to achieve the minimum acceptable standard. Frequencies of all activities, including those undertaken irregularly or on a periodic basis, need to be specified.

Managing equipment and materials

Facilities service operations involve not only the input of human resources, but also the input of materials, equipment and commodities. The types and significance of these resources varies considerably from one service sub-division to the next. For example, in the cleaning and housekeeping service operation, cleaning agents, equipment and other supplies need to be purchased. In this context on-going materials costs are usually no more than 10 per cent of the total operating cost. Of a large budget, 10 per cent can itself be a considerable figure, but it is the impact which this 10 per cent of the cost has on the other 90 per cent (the labour), which is of significance. Cleaning and housekeeping require little capital investment in major pieces of equipment compared to catering and laundry services. Without the appropriate materials and supplies available at the right time, in the right quantities and in the right place, labour costs can rise significantly, as staff try to 'make do' and quality is likely to suffer. The knock on costs of not having sufficient material resources will be much greater than the costs involved in implementing and maintaining an efficient materials management system. Linen shortages may reduce room availability and, thus, impact on rooms revenue. Where supplies are short, staff may borrow from other work areas or worse still, in the case of cleaning, bring in their own items from home. This can also impact on the achievement of the standard of quality and consistency besides constituting a possible safety, fire or hygiene risk. On the other hand, excessive stocks are unnecessarily expensive, reduce cash flow, take up storage space and constitute an increased safety or fire hazard.

Effective materials management

This should ensure that, at the lowest possible cost:

- the correct items are available at the point of usage
- a continuity of supply is maintained
- stock items are maintained in good condition in storage
- stocks are stored securely
- standardization of supplies is maintained

- supplies are correctly used and usage is monitored
- supplies are evaluated
- information on new products and supplies is acquired
- minimum stock levels are maintained.

Whatever the nature and purpose of the equipment and material resources, they should be available when required. The simplest way to ensure availability is to hold them in stock. However, this costs money in terms of wastage and obsolescence, provision of storage space and the lost opportunity cost of this, provision of security measures and loss of interest on finances tied up in the stock. These 'holding costs', as they are known, have to be accounted for on the balance sheet. Overstocking may very easily occur. However, as already inferred, materials not available will also incur costs which, in the worst case scenario, could lead to loss of sales. Keeping materials in stock acts as a buffer between the rate of replenishment and the rate of depletion.

Consumable resources (those used up on an on-going basis, but in relatively small quantities) are often purchased in bulk to take account of economies in scale and suppliers discount structures.

Deliveries inward should ideally be planned so that stocks are replenished just as the last item is withdrawn from the stores. Accurate management information is required on which to base replenishment forecasts. This task is compounded where supply or demand is uncertain or where the latter varies greatly. It may be necessary to build an extra stock level as a safety precaution, but this should be as a last resort due to cost implications.

Replenishment and depletion may be either an intermittent activity, where materials are taken into or out of stock at intervals (e.g. weekly or fortnightly), or a continuous activity, where there is a constant flow of material into and out of stock (e.g. in a dry commodity store within a catering outlet). The key questions to be asked are as follows.

- How much stock should be carried to ensure that material is available when it is wanted?
- How often should replenishment occur?

There are a number of ways to determine replenishment rates and order size, including economic order quantity, fixed order cycle/topping up or imprest and the fixed order point systems.

Inventory control

An efficient inventory control system is crucial to the effective running of the service operation. The system itself must be cost effective.

Orders initiated by the stores department are usually sent by an administration department and include details of items and quantities required from the defined supplier. When goods are delivered, the accompanying delivery note must be signed with a copy returned to the supplier to generate an invoice for payment and one sent to the finance department as an authority to pay when the invoice is received. Goods received should immediately be checked off against the order and also physically checked for quality and quantity so that defective items (ullages) can be returned to the supplier immediately and measures taken to rectify discrepancies in quantity. Alternatively, this activity could be conducted by the supplier on delivery.

When goods have been accepted by the storekeeper, receipt details are recorded either in the goods received book or the computer equivalent. The items are then stored as appropriate. Stores areas are fire risks because of the nature of some of the products stored, but also due to their infrequent access. Items must be stored in appropriate conditions and temperature, ventilation and lighting should be controlled as required. Items must also be stored in a manner which will facilitate retrieval for use and enable efficient stock rotation.

Bin cards (manual or computerized) are frequently used as a means of keeping a quick check of current stock. They provide data on usage which is necessary for calculating order levels. Bin cards are also useful if periodic stocktaking forms part of the control process, when actual stock on the shelves should tally with the bin card. Stock in use should also be accounted for.

Pareto analysis

Pareto analysis or ABC analysis seeks to identify those stock items that make the largest contribution to inventory value and, thus, where close control will have the greatest impact on total annual usage costs. It is normally found that 80 per cent of inventory costs is incurred by 20 per cent of items. This 20 per cent of items needs to be targeted with a view to reviewing specification, source of supply, purchasing arrangements, storage, distribution and usage. To be more specific, this approach normally identifies three groups A, B and C and is further explained in Figure 5.3.

Computerized inventory control

The whole inventory control process can now be computerized. There are many software packages on the market. Orders, product prices and costs, Pareto analysis, bin cards, product specifications, details of hazardous substances, goods received and issues, ullages and budget details can all be recorded.

Control of hazardous substances

There are many chemicals used within facilities service operations, particularly housekeeping, which could constitute a health risk. Some substances are toxic, corrosive, irritant or flammable. Some cause skin irritation, whilst others produce irritating fumes or are poisonous. Housekeeping supplies which are classed as hazardous substances are:

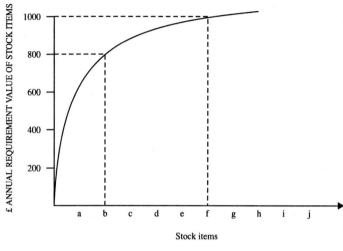

Key
a neutral detergent
b disposable towels   80% total costs = 20% of products (2 items)

c disposable cloths
d non abrasive cleaning paste
e abrasive hand pads   15% total costs = 40% of products (4 items)
f alkali detergent

g abrasive floor pads
h water-based polish   5% total costs = 40% of products (4 items)
i rubber gloves
j mop heads

Figure 5.3 Pareto curve showing comparative annual value of stock items.

- acids (e.g. toilet cleansers and concrete etching chemicals)
- toxics (e.g. stain removers)
- flammables (e.g. solvent-based polishes and seals and chewing gum remover)
- alkalis (e.g. alkali detergents used for stripping water-based polish applications)
- chemical disinfectants (e.g. hypochlorides).

In the UK, the Control of Substances Hazardous to Health Regulations (1994), part of the Health and Safety at Work Act 1974 have implications. For legal as well as safety reasons, where such substances are deemed necessary to be used, they should be easily identified as hazardous and records kept of:

- the name, stores record number and any synonym
- the ingredients and physical properties
- the supplier and details of supplier's hazardous data sheet
- the issues made and items returned
- the procedures for their safe use.

Stock distribution and issue

Options include:

- new for old or counter-exchange, where the old item must be returned before a replacement is given
- topping up or imprest system, where each store area has a pre-determined stock level and items are topped up to this level at a pre-determined frequency (e.g. daily or weekly)
- set amount, where a set quantity of stock is determined for each area store and that amount is issued at a prescribed frequency (alternatively, the container from the last delivery can be removed, thus retrieving the remaining stock and replacing it with a new delivery)
- requisition, where users complete a requisition for the items they require and items are either delivered or users collect them from the stores.

Often a combination of systems is used, depending on the items and the situation. The main aims of a stock distribution system is to facilitate inventory control by:

- ensuring that sufficient items are available for operatives at the right time and in the right place

- minimizing time wasted due to insufficient supplies or broken equipment
- minimizing labour and time spent on stores matters
- ensuring that deviations to normal usage patterns are detected quickly, investigated and remedied
- preventing pilferage and wastage
- providing information for budgetary control and evaluation purposes.

Equipment

Equipment scheduling

Scheduling helps equipment, particularly expensive capital equipment, to be used efficiently. It reduces waiting time when equipment is being used elsewhere, being transported or receiving maintenance. Scheduling of work also ensures that equipment is used to its full capacity, never overloaded and minimizes unproductive time.

If, for example, a floor maintenance machine is shared between two areas, then the scrubbing operation must be scheduled at different times in each area. If one set of cleaning equipment is to be shared by two members of staff in one work area, then work must be scheduled in such a way as to avoid both employees requiring the same equipment at the same time. It may be more cost effective and efficient in the long run to purchase minimum quantities of equipment, particularly large-scale capital equipment, and schedule optimum usage supported by planned preventative maintenance. As long as the system incorporates a planned replacement cycle, new state-of-the-art equipment can be purchased (or hired) more often than purchasing more equipment which is used less and therefore lasts for a longer period before replacement is required. However, it is false economy to skimp on equipment purchase. In most facilities services operations where capital equipment represents only a small proportion of the budget compared with labour, lack of equipment availability can adversely affect productivity. In catering and laundry services where high capital investment is required, equipment capacity and task duration will have a significant impact on equipment scheduling.

Equipment control

Large-scale equipment, including dry suction cleaners, floor maintenance machines and laundry and cooking equipment, also needs to be controlled. It is useful to maintain a record on each item recording details such as:

- supplier
- price
- any accessories purchased
- serial number
- date it was commissioned and condemned
- location of usage
- details and dates of maintenance and electrical testing, repair and spare parts required.

Such information is vital for equipment evaluation, particularly when considering replacement of the item and assessing depreciation. Details of electrical testing are required by the Electricity at Work Regulations 1989 and the Health and Safety at Work Act 1974. Planned replacement cycles should be introduced for all large-scale equipment.

Estimating staffing levels

The preceding stages and decisions provide a sound basis for estimating required staffing levels, designing individual jobs, allocating work and subsequently deploying staff to fulfil the service specification or service level agreement. Efficiency and cost effectiveness are key principles at this stage.

The main aim is to establish an optimum staffing level. Too many staff will result in higher than necessary labour costs, with possibly too much time available to do too little work or too frequent repetition of work. Too few staff can result in stress, fatigue, low morale, high labour turnover and high accident rates. Both too high and too few staff can result in poor standards of service and customer contact and can subsequently lead to customer and staff dissatisfaction.

In operations where it is difficult to estimate demand or where demand fluctuates, staffing levels must be flexible enough to respond to these patterns. For example, flexi-time, job sharing, recruiting temporary or agency staff, hiring additional part-time staff or contracting out excess demand are all options to be considered. Another strategy to consider is interchangeability of operational staff through multi-skilling and job rotation.

It is more effective to have a model or formula as a basis for estimating staffing levels and each type of facilities service will have a typical formula or model to follow. However, some general principles, as detailed under 'Work measurement' apply. Software packages are available for estimating some facilities services staffing levels.

Work measurement

The service specification or definition provides the basis for work measurement. Work measurement involves quantifying the time involved in performing the tasks, activities and services which comprise the service to be offered. Work measurement methods include:

- using past experience
- experimentation
- undertaking crude time studies

- scientific work study approaches
- using published synthetic time values.

The latter are devised through method time measurement techniques, whereby tasks are broken down into basic motions which have already been measured and given pre-determined time values. The time values for all motions can then be built up for a particular task without it having to be observed. In other words, the time value for a task is synthesized. Some organizations commission work study or use method time measurement techniques to produce standard time values for use throughout the whole of the organization. Such data may not be appropriate for application in different types of organizations. Usage patterns, area density and agreed times of availability and/or delivery will all influence the estimation of work hours.

Work study or synthetic time values are based on the actual working time required to undertake the job. Various allowances must be taken into account in the final calculations, including time for:

- collecting supplies, getting started at the beginning of the shift, putting things away and cleaning down at the end of the shift
- natural breaks, working more slowly near the end of a shift or working in hot or cold conditions
- meal and beverage breaks
- holidays and bank holiday lieu days cover
- sickness and absence cover.

Allowances are determined by company policy and are normally incorporated into the final calculation on a percentage basis (e.g. 10 per cent contingency allowance for equipment preparation and relaxation purposes).

In some organizations, the staffing requirement is expressed as a full-time or whole-time equivalent rather than as a total number of working hours required for a defined period, such as a week or a year. The full-time or whole-time equivalent is calculated by dividing the total number of working hours required, for example, per week (including the allowances) by the number of hours worked by a full-time member of staff per week, as defined by company policy. This is known as the 'establishment figure'. In reality, a mix of full-time and part-time staff are probably employed and, therefore, the total number of working hours required per week or per year is a more meaningful figure.

An experienced estimator, particularly in a contracting situation, will be able to short cut such a detailed analysis and rely on a series of norms built up over time and relevant to a particular type of operation. For example, a cleaning contractor may estimate on a basis of $50m^2$ per hour to clean offices or $10m^2$ per hour to clean sanitary areas.

Job design

When designing a job, it is necessary to consider the range of tasks, activities and services to be allocated to an individual. This will be influenced by the nature of the service operation, type of organization and its objectives, the standards of quality to be achieved and the expected capabilities of the staff. Provision may be made for individuals or groups of staff to undertake a particular range of tasks, activities or services as required (e.g. a room attendant allocated to a specific section of bedrooms or a catering assistant to a particular food outlet).

Staff may be allocated either on a permanent or a rotational basis to a team, a range of tasks and activities or a specific section or location within the organization. Rotation often occurs within service operations where some of the workload is boring, repetitive, strenuous, unpleasant or costed at a different rate. Rotation also occurs across service operations to achieve multi-skilling of staff. For example, staff in an hotel may rotate from housekeeping to food service to bar duties or they may rotate within operations (e.g. from electrical to fitting to plumbing duties).

The specific tasks and activities to be allocated to a specific grade of staff and job title will need to be determined. Demarcation disputes and inflexibility occurs where a larger variety of grades cover specific activities. Fewer grades encourages multi-skilling and increases flexibility and efficiency gain. At one time, most large hotels employed a full brigade of front office personnel with specialist staff in reservations, reception, bookkeeping and cashiering functions and team leaders in each area. Nowadays, influenced by the advent of technology, multi-skilled reception staff can cover the whole range of front office duties. Days off, holidays, sickness and absence are also much easier to cover.

These job design decisions affect work allocation, scheduling, shift hours and the mix of part-time and full-time staff required. Job descriptions can be devised for each grade of staff or area of responsibility defined. A job description is a broad statement of the purpose, scope, duties and responsibilities of a particular job. It may also explain the environment in which the job will be undertaken and the lines of communication and responsibility.

Scheduling

Activity scheduling is concerned with ordering events within the operating system and taking decisions about when specific resources, including staffing levels and the movement of materials and equipment, are needed. There are four key aspects of activity scheduling to be considered, namely task duration, frequency, sequence and timing. Task duration and task frequency have already been discussed (see pages 151 and 142 respectively).

Task sequence

The order in which tasks should be carried out depends on the rationale for the whole job of which the task forms a part.

Many factors, which vary from operation to operation, influence the ordering of events, including:

- certain tasks may have to be undertaken at specific times as dictated by other suppliers' or service providers' routines or availability (e.g. scheduling cleaning activities after redecoration is influenced by completion time on the part of the maintenance team)
- some tasks will need to be undertaken prior to or after others (e.g. dry suction cleaning of floors should occur after bedmaking or mop sweeping prior to damp mopping)
- certain jobs may involve two staff working together (e.g. lifting and carrying heavy items, using ladders, floor scrubbing and drying and making double beds).

Task timing

Determining when tasks should be carried out may be customer driven (e.g. defined within the service specification or service level agreement) and/or determined by demand and usage patterns. Alternatively, timing of tasks may be system-driven, in terms of a particular input being required at a particular time. 'Front line' service operations normally fall into the former and 'back room' activities into the latter.

Parallel engineering and just in time approaches may be considered here. The parallel engineering approach involves planning all the functions involved in a process at the beginning rather than planning each function after the previous one has become operational. Hence, the suggestion here that the design of the monitoring and quality assurance system should be considered at the service specification or service level agreement stage and be an integral part of the delivery system rather than be considered after the delivery system is operational.

The just in time philosophy sets out to improve overall system productivity through the elimination of waste and enhancement of overall service quality. Its origins lie in delivering resource materials and/or finished goods in the right quantities, at the right times, in the right places and using minimal resources.

Deployment and coverage

Work schedules

Work can be allocated to individuals or small groups by means of a work schedule. A work schedule is defined as a timetable of tasks to be undertaken by each individual worker within a certain period of time or shift. Carefully planned work schedules should incorporate:

- a list of tasks or activities to be completed (in some situations, these will be prioritized)
- the sequence in which these tasks or activities should be completed
- the approximate times at which tasks or activities should be undertaken and the amount of time allocated
- the break times allocated
- any special factors (e.g. security arrangements)
- hours of duty or shift hours.

A work schedule should ensure that an individual knows exactly what to do, and where and when to do it. This avoids worry, confusion and fatigue. It also ensures that all tasks, whether daily, weekly or periodic, are covered with none missed out or duplicated. Each individual should be given a fair and even distribution of work within the number of hours to be worked, with no overlapping of duties. Time should be saved as in conjunction with induction and training, staff should not be waiting around for instructions. Equipment may also be scheduled to ensure a fair and even distribution and allow even wear and tear.

Team leaders will know where staff are at a given time and which area or tasks can be checked off. Work schedules are useful when a relief member of staff is covering an area, as a training aid and to help set standards of quality by ensuring that an appropriate amount of time to undertake the job is allocated and the correct sequencing occurs.

By plotting on a time plan, such as a Gantt chart, those tasks which can only be performed at certain times, those tasks which have to be completed before a deadline or prior to another task and meal and beverage breaks, and then fitting in the other tasks, it is possible to highlight peaks and troughs in activity. This helps to determine when periodic tasks can be inserted and so identify the shift hours when staff are required – establishing the mix of part-time and full-time staff needed in a particular area.

Rostering

Staff must be on duty to undertake the tasks and services specified in the service specification or service level agreement at the appropriate times. This will involve rostering staff to cover all areas as and when required, but at the same time planning for staff to have their off-duty allocation on a fair and rational basis. Relief staff will be required to cover when a seven-day service is required. This might involve a full-time member of staff working five days and a part-time member of staff working two days or, alternatively, two part-time members of staff working three and four days respectively. Rostering involves preparing a duty rota which indicates on a weekly or even monthly basis which staff are on duty and which are off duty and which areas of work are to be covered by named staff.

When preparing a duty rota, the needs of both the staff and the organization must be considered. The following are some of the options to consider when planning rotas.

- A fixed rota, where an individual works the same hours and days every week. Their rest days may or may not be covered, depending on whether a five- or seven-day service is required.
- A rotating days off rota, where the days off rotate each week. So, for example, an individual would have Monday and Tuesday in week 1 and Wednesday and Thursday in week 2. The staff have to work no more than seven days before having a day off. However, in the future, legislation could be introduced which requires this practice to be changed. Alternatively, rotation may be based on the first day off with an individual having Monday and Tuesday in week 1 and then Tuesday and Wednesday in week 2. This system usually applies when staff work the same shift hours every day.
- An alternating shift rota, where staff cover different shifts each day. For example, an early shift one day and a late shift the next day or early shift on day 1, middle shift on day 2 and late shift on day 3. In this system, staff may have worked a late shift one day and be expected to work an early shift the next day. A financial allowance is sometimes awarded for working alternating shift patterns.

In some cases, staff are expected to work split shifts. This may not be popular, particularly when staff live out as they may not have time to go home between shifts and it involves double travel expenses and time. A split shift allowance may be an incentive. It is probably more economical to appoint two part-time members of staff in this situation.

Duty rotas should be documented and communicated to staff well in advance, so they can plan around their days off. A systematic cycle such as alternate weekends off when a seven-day coverage is required will simplify arrangements and facilitate planning. Often a relief pool of staff is required and specific relief staff are allocated to cover days off in a particular area, so becoming a 'permanent' relief and, thus, part of the team for that area of work.

Usage and occupancy trends and service demand will influence the rostering system adopted. There is a tendency where demand fluctuates to employ part-time staff rather than full-time staff to increase flexibility. In circumstances where enhanced payments are made for shift or weekend coverage, lower priority tasks and weekly and periodic tasks should be covered when lower pay rates are applicable.

In some organizations a pool of non-allocated hours are kept available to employ relief staff to cover holidays and bank holiday entitlements. Again, a fair and rational system for allocating and covering holiday entitlements should be implemented.

Organizational structure and team culture

The organizational structure required to enable the facilities services operation to be managed and delivered will be influenced by all the preceding components of the delivery system and the specific decisions made about each one. Certainly, the size and scope of the total service and the number and nature of service sub-divisions will influence the shape of the required infra-structure. Other influences will include:

- the geographical location of the organization's building stock
- the location of dedicated areas of operation
- the perceived need for technical and specialized versus generic management skills and competencies
- the centralization or decentralization of decision-making philosophy to be adopted
- the nature of the culture desired in terms of quality, responsiveness to change and empowerment of staff
- the management and leadership styles to be adopted – whether consultative or autocratic. A consultative management style encouraging staff participation and

empowerment through team briefings and quality circles will involve staff in solving their own problems, self-appraisal and continuous review of service delivery improvement and, generally, participation in the decision-making process.

Outputs

The nature of the primary and secondary outputs

Decisions made about each of the components just listed will affect the nature of the end product or output and its delivery. The end product, of course, must be consonant with the service specification or service level agreement and satisfy the customers' requirements. In facilities management, the primary output will be a package comprising both tangible products and service elements. A secondary output (i.e. waste) will be created in this context (see page 162).

Establishing standards

The factors which contribute to this are identified in Figure 5.4. The specific decisions made about each delivery system component will also contribute to the setting of standards. The definition of standards is developed in Chapter 7.

The delivery specification

Once the delivery system has been designed following the developmental and decision-making process outlined earlier, the specific decisions made can be translated into a delivery specification. This delivery specification would, in fact, form the basis of a tender submission by either the in-house provider

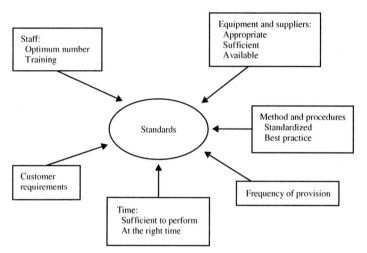

Figure 5.4 Contributors to setting standards.

or an external contractor in a contracting situation. A delivery specification for the housekeeping service would typically include:

- the physical areas to be covered, coded by:
  - individual rooms and numbers
  - room types and quantities of each, particularly where each room type is the same or similar in size and design
- the tasks, activities and services to be performed, including specification of standard methods of performance and, thus, equipment and agents to be used and standards to be achieved
- frequencies of each task, activity and service
- coded standard procedures for each room type, including tasks, frequencies and time allocations
- the total number of staffing hours
- deployment of staff, coverage of areas and rostering
- duties of individual members of staff
- supervision and management cover.

Implementation

Implementation of the delivery system is key to achieving the desired results. Involving existing staff in the design and decision-making process and, subsequently, in continuous review and improvement is essential. First, staff working at the 'sharp end' are likely to be more knowledgable about practicalities and obstacles. Second, involvement will encourage ownership of the system and motivate. Implementation must be supported by effective briefings and training. Evaluation and feedback, responsiveness and adaptability are also critical factors.

Monitoring and control

To ensure consistency of quality and achievement, delivery must be monitored and controlled. This aspect is the subject of Chapter 7.

Waste disposal

The Health and Safety at Work Act 1974, under the 'duty of care' requires all reasonable steps to be taken to manage any waste generated by an organization and prevent its illegal disposal by others. Unlimited fines can be imposed for breaking the law. With the raising of awareness of environmental issues, particularly through the media and legislation, hotels need to consider ways of minimizing waste creation. This will, in turn, have a knock on effect on cost.

Before waste can be disposed of, it needs to be collected. To manage this process, an analysis needs to be made of all the areas producing waste and the type and quantity of waste generated in each area. Different waste types require different collection, storage and disposal arrangements and the volumes

of each type might affect decisions on equipment requirements (e.g. the need for shredders and compactors). Also,
corporate policy on recycling will affect collection as this process usually involves segregation at source (using different
containers for different groups of waste). Economic factors as
well as ethic values will influence decisions on recycling, whilst
some income can be generated by this process and savings
made by reducing the volume of waste to be disposed of, sort-
ing and separate storage does have cost implications. The main
categories of waste generated by an hotel are listed in Table
5.2.

To choose suitable containers for waste needs consideration of issues such as the ability to contain liquid waste, the
flammability of the waste, the exclusion of vermin and flies,

Table 5.2 Categories of waste generated in an hotel

Category of waste	Types of waste
Kitchen waste	Food
	Tins and packaging
Bar waste	Bottles and cans
General waste	Litter, dirt and waste paper
Sanitary waste	Effluent
	Paper and sanitary towels
Cleaning waste	Aerosols
	Plastic containers
	Suction cleaner bags
	Used equipment (e.g. mop heads and cleaning cloths)
Sharps	Razor blades
Fuel emission	Carbon dioxide, oxides of nitrogen
Scrap	Furniture
	Equipment
	Electrical apparatus
Office waste	Paper
	Toner cartridges

prevention of scattering by the wind and the ability to be kept clean. These factors apply to collecting the waste at source and holding the waste in the allocated storage area. Most waste needs to be stored prior to collection by contractors or local authority units. Another factor to address is the frequency of emptying containers at source and collection from the central collection point.

References and further reading

Axler, B.H. (1976) *Management of Hospitality Operations.* Bobbs-Merrill.

Henley Distance Learning Ltd. (1991) *Managing Operations.*

Kasavana, M.L. and Brooks, R.M. (1995) *Managing Front Office Operations* (4th edn). Educational Institute of the American Hotel and Motel Association.

Whittle, S. and Foster, M. (1991) In *Managing Operations.* Henley Distance Learning Ltd.

Research (Harvey-Jones, 1995) indicates that there is an enormously under-utilized resource in the capability of staff in organizations.

People are the most important asset of any organization as the effective use of other assets depends on them, particularly at a time when organizations are struggling to survive, cope with unprecedented rates of change and strive for greater efficiencies and, thus, growth. People are agents of change and the key to giving an organization its competitive edge. Commitment to the Investors in People standard itself is not necessary to develop staff to achieve business objectives, review training and development needs, design and implement training and development programmes throughout employment and evaluate this investment in order to achieve improved effectiveness. This philosophy must be embedded in an organization's mission and become part of its culture for its long-term survival.

The cost of human resources

In many organizations, particularly hospitality organizations, facilities services are not only labour intensive, but also large in terms of numbers of staff employed. Often, staffing comprises somewhere in the region of 90 per cent of the total service operations budget. Given the proportional significance of the facilities services staffing budget, more scope exists for increasing operational efficiencies in this area than in many others. Hence, the consideration of compulsory competitive tendering and outsourcing strategies in this area (see Chapter 4).

It is essential, but not always easy, to isolate and continually monitor the facilities services staffing costs within the overall organization's budget. Sub-sets of the staffing budget (e.g. housekeeping and cleaning, maintenance, portering, security, supervision and management) must also be monitored and variances from the norm analysed when necessary.

6
Investing in staff

Aims and objectives

This chapter aims to:

- stress the importance and cost of the human resource to organizations
- identify the characteristics of a learning organization
- define the aims and purpose of training and development and explore some issues to be considered at each stage of the training and development cycle
- emphasize the importance of evaluating training and development, including cost benefit analysis
- introduce National Vocational Qualifications (NVQs) and the infra-structure required to offer in-house assessment to staff
- consider the significance of mentoring as a staff support mechanism
- identify the value of adopting a staff care and welfare policy and the characteristics of such a policy.

The importance of the human resource

Commitment to the Investors in People standard helps organizations to improve the performance by releasing the full potential of staff to contribute to the organization's success. It focuses on people and their working performance.

Costs associated with the human resource budget include staff pay, the costs of recruitment, training and development, labour turnover, workwear, meals on duty and paid breaks.

Changing patterns of work

The changes which are affecting organizations and how people work within them are outlined in Table 2.1. In accommodating these changes, many organizations are cutting back, reducing staffing levels and reorganizing. Consequently, there are fewer jobs available and more people in the labour pool. Some hotel chains are shedding their general management and developing a regional management approach. Some hotels are diversifying and offering a greater range of services and packages (e.g. day lets from 9 am to 5 pm for travellers). Other hotels are reducing the level of service offered and transferring this function to the customer (e.g. in budget hotels targeted at travellers staying one night only and located in close proximity to a chain restaurant and in motels catering for tourists, with vending machines on each corridor).

Research (Association of Graduate Recruiters, 1995) shows that career patterns are changing and that the 'job for life' with its planned career structure is disappearing as is the clear functional identity and the progressive rise in income and security. This will change the 'psychological contract' between employer and employee which in the past has involved staff offering loyalty and skills in return for security and job stability. This is being replaced by a culture which is customer- and client-focused, more environmentally and ethically aware and based on portfolio careers, project management, homeworking, flatter structures, leaderless teams, adding value, lifelong learning and the need to stay employable. In sum, a culture where the onus is on the individual to manage his or her relationship with work.

With the decline in the number of school leavers, there are now fewer young people entering the labour market. Alternative sources of labour have to be explored, including part-time workers, women returners and older members of society. Working patterns and routines have to change to accommodate the needs and capabilities of these alternative groups.

Human resource strategies which include succession planning – where individuals are developed to take over specific responsibilities when the current post-holder leaves *and* the competencies required by staff in the future are determined – need to be part of an organization's long-term strategic plan.

New skills

It is apparent from this and from the changing organizational needs highlighted in Chapter 1, that people need new skills to cope with these changing demands in the workplace. Research has identified the skills and attributes required, particularly by graduates, in the twenty-first century. These 'self-reliance' skills as they have been called are outlined in Table 6.1 and

Table 6.1 Self-reliance skills

Self-awareness
Self-promotion
Exploring and creating opportunities
Action planning
Networking
Matching and decision-making
Negotiation
Political awareness
Coping with uncertainty
Development focus
Transfer skills
Self-confidence

(Adapted from Association of Graduate Recruiters, 1995)

their applicability for all levels of staff is worthy of consideration.

Certainly, future managers will need additional skills to manage constant uncertainty and change. As knowledge and skills soon become obsolete, the need for effective learning skills assumes greater importance. Lifelong learning becomes essential for survival.

The learning organization

Organizations need to be flexible, responsive and responsible as the opportunities and threats they are confronted with are increasing in quantity, intensity and influence (Swieringa and Wierdsman, 1992). The concept of the 'learning organization' or 'learning company' is based on the premise that the culture of an organization can be changed through the learning and development of its staff. A learning organization has been defined as one which 'facilitates the learning of all its members and consciously transforms itself and its context' (Pedler et al., 1997: 3).

Organizational learning unlocks the potential in an organization by defining an attitude and a set of principles to motivate, educate and guide individuals and teams. Through the learning process, staff not only acquire, assimilate, adapt, develop and apply knowledge, but they are empowered to question and challenge assumptions, actions, procedures and processes and, thus, to stimulate change and make improvements. This enables organizations to handle continuous and rapid change more effectively. It is particularly powerful where individuals collaborate in a collective learning process within a team and cascade their learning to other teams in the organization. The collective intelligence of the staff is a very important organizational asset. A culture where individuals are encouraged to be genuinely concerned for one another, are able to build relationships based on trust and can disclose and share information in a non-threatening environment can be perceived as a competitive advantage.

A learning organization is not easy to achieve and can take some time. It cannot operate effectively within a power-driven culture.

Teams

There is an increasing emphasis on achieving results through teams rather than managing people on a one-to-one basis. Groups create a synergy, whereby the group can be more effective than the individuals within it. Groups can work more effectively to solve more complex problems, make better decisions, release more creativity and do more to build individual skills and commitment (Blanchard *et al.*, 1996).

Teams develop through four identifiable stages, commonly referred to as:

1   forming or orientation
2   storming or dissatisfaction and conflict
3   norming or resolution and building
4   performing or production.

The leader's role changes from managing to facilitating and educating, and involves:

- responsibility for:
  - task functions (i.e. getting the job done)
  - group maintenance functions (i.e. developing and maintaining harmony and cohesion)
- leading the group according to the stage of group development and group needs (known as 'situational leadership'); the change in leadership style required can be plotted against the four stages of group development (see Table 6.2).

Table 6.2 Changing leadership styles

Group stage	Leadership style
Orientation	Directing
	Highly directive and not very supportive
Dissatisfaction	Coaching
	Highly directive and highly supportive
Resolution	Supporting
	Highly supportive but not very directive
Production	Delegating
	Not very supportive and not very directive

(Adapted from Blanchard *et al.*, 1996)

The leader has to be able to 'let go' and share control for the team to become self-directed and empowered.

Six PERFORM characteristics of high performing teams have been identified by Blanchard *et al.* (1996) and they are described in Table 6.3.

Training and development

Supporting people through change and releasing their full potential means recognizing and meeting the needs of both individuals and teams. Organizations need to consider their training and development philosophy and approach and focus on how organizational learning principles and methodologies can be developed. The training and development policy statement, which will clarify and promote executive commitment, should address:

- the aims and purpose of the training and development
- specific objectives, outcomes and priorities

Table 6.3 Characteristics of effective teams

Anagram	Characteristic	Description
P	Purpose	Sharing Commitment to a common purpose Clear goals, roles and strategies
E	Empowerment	Confidence Sharing responsibility Supportive and respectful Policies and practices to support objectives Access to collective skills and resource base
R	Relationships and communications	Openness and honesty Warmth, understanding and acceptance Value different opinions and perspectives Actively listen to each other
F	Flexibility	Take on different roles as necessary Sharing responsibility for leadership and roles Adaptable to changing demands Explore alternative ideas and options
O	Optimal productivity	High output Excellent quality Effective decision-making Clear problem-solving
R	Recognition and appreciation	Of individuals and team Feel respected and valued
M	Morale	Feel good Confidence and motivation Pride and satisfaction Team spirit and sense of belonging

(Adapted from Blanchard et al., 1996)

- the scope of training and development within the organization and recommended practices (e.g. NVQs, distance learning and day release)
- employee eligibility and equality of opportunity for all employees
- the responsibilities of employer and employees
- the resources to be allocated, in terms of people, facilities and finance
- the means of monitoring and evaluation.

Training and development is usually required in response to some event, such as:

- the appointment of a new employee
- the implementation of the Investors in People standard and the subsequent introduction of a staff development plan
- the installation of new equipment (e.g. a hyperspeed floor maintenance machine) or technology (e.g. computerization)
- the introduction of a new product (e.g. neutral detergent or computer package)
- a change in working method or practice
- a complaint or accident
- the need for multi-skilling
- the introduction of new legislation or codes of practice
- the introduction of a new philosophy or organizational principle.

Aims and purpose of training and development

Training and development should be directly related to the business's goals, targets and key result areas at individual, team and organizational level. There is a direct link between training and development and commercial success (MSC, 1981). Learning is at the heart of the training and development process and it is about changing behaviour. Learning is a cyclical process, the stages of which are highlighted in Figure 6.1.

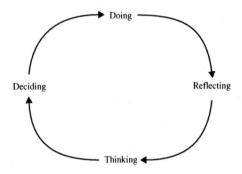

Figure 6.1 Kolb's learning cycle.

To explain the cycle, an individual gains experience through undertaking an activity. He or she reflects on the experience and attempts to understand the experience through analysis and conceptualization. Then the individual makes choices and decides on the next steps and the cycle repeats itself. According to Kolb's approach, learning is never-ending and the process is constantly repeated.

For example, if a new front office IT package were introduced, receptionists (after some training) would use it for the first time (doing). They would reflect on this new experiences in terms of what they did, how they did it, what went well and what they were unsure about (reflecting). They would then think about how they would have to change the way they work, analysing how it would impact on the tasks they and others perform, what they would need to do to improve their skills to be more effective and so on (thinking). They would then make decisions about how to do it next time (deciding) and the learning cycle would start again.

There are many other benefits of training and development, including:

- improved performance
- increased productivity
- higher quality output or throughput

- lower wastage
- reduced labour turnover
- increased morale
- fewer accidents
- fewer complaints
- reduced absenteeism and sickness
- multi-skilling and greater flexibility
- improved talent identification
- improved cooperation and relationships
- improved health, safety and hygiene
- improved security
- energy conservation
- realization of potential
- development of lifelong learning skills
- development of reflective practitioners (i.e. staff reflect on and learn from experience and use this learning to improve future practice).

The training and development cycle

This cycle involves the following stages:

- identifying the training and development needs
- identifying the target population
- setting objectives and priorities
- designing the training and development programme
- delivering the training and development
- evaluating the results.

All those involved in the training and development cycle need to know and understand the business objectives, targets and key result areas of the business. They must also be aware of the external forces which may effect changes to the business plan and the internal culture and sub-cultures of the organization which may prevent training and development being effective.

Identifying the training and development needs

A training and development needs analysis involves identifying the essential skills, knowledge and experience (i.e. those key skills and competencies that are required for meeting the business's objectives now and in the future). These are then matched by means of an audit to the competencies which individuals and groups possess to identify the gaps and discrepancies in performance that exist in reality between what staff are capable of doing now, what they should be doing and what will be required of them in the future. This identification of training needs provides the basis of a personal development plan for the individual and the training and development plan. The needs of both individuals and groups should be monitored as part of an on-going review process.

Analysis of training needs also involves determining how these needs might be met within the realities of the resources available and the organizational culture.

Identifying the target population

To identify the target population, it has to be established which individuals and groups really need training and a priority order then has to be set.

Setting objectives, outcomes and priorities

It is necessary to determine a priority order of the knowledge, understanding, skills and attitudes which need improvement and set SMART objectives for the training and development. That is objectives which are S(specific), M(measurable), A(attainable), R(realistic) and T(time specific).

Designing the training and development programme

The training and development programme is derived from the organization's business plan and training and development needs analysis. It involves deciding what sort of training will achieve the business's objectives and the desired behaviour required as a result of the training. Desired behaviour might include the acquisition of improved understanding, new knowledge or new skills, application of existing knowledge to new situations or problems, changed attitudes and behaviours or a combination of these.

Decisions will have to be made with regard to:

- the content to be covered in order to meet the business's objectives
- the outcomes to be achieved
- the targets to be met
- the roles and responsibilities of employers, employees and trainers
- the timescale in which the training and development must be accomplished
- training and development methods and practices to be employed (e.g. workshops, seminars, visiting speakers, demonstrations, case studies, problem-solving exercises, distance learning packages or computer-aided learning)
- supply and delivery, in terms of college or university programmes, training provider workshops, conferences, in-house sessions and on the job training
- the resources required and available in-house (including accommodation)
- the evaluation criteria and processes to be used.

Induction

Induction is the introduction of a new employee to the organization and its objectives and policies, to the working

environment, working practices and procedures and to existing staff. The purpose of the induction process is to relieve
anxiety and provide the new member of staff with a good
understanding of the organization. It should be designed to
help new staff settle in and quickly feel part of the organization, enabling them to develop confidence and contribute to
the organization more speedily.

Induction is beneficial not only as a basis for formulating
relationships and communication links but also as a way of
reducing labour turnover. Many staff leave their new
employment after a relatively short period of time (e.g. a
few days to a few weeks). This is an expensive burden for
any operation. A well-planned and well-executed induction
programme should help to prevent this happening as it helps
to create a good first impression, which can encourage staff
to stay longer. Induction is the first stage in a successful
retention process.

Induction may be in two or three stages. The first stage is
the induction to the work environment, the actual work to be
undertaken, standards of performance to be achieved and colleagues. This will be undertaken by the specific service operation within which the new member of staff is to work. It is
sometimes referred to as the immediate or psychological induction. In a large organization and one where facilities services
are integrated within one division, there may be a second
induction stage to introduce new staff to issues such as health
and safety, customer care, and fire and accident procedures,
which are common to all facilities services staff. The second
induction stage is usually organized at divisional level.

The third induction stage involves providing background
information to the wider context of the whole organization,
its business objectives, structure, policies and conditions of
service. This is usually organized by the human resources or
training and development division and may be undertaken a
while after the new employee has started and settled in. It often
involves a cross-section of staff from the organization.

The content of a typical first stage induction programme is

contained in Table 6.4. It includes the administration which has to be undertaken by the human resources division. The order of priority and sequencing will vary according to the level and number of staff being inducted at any one time. Many organizations provide new staff with a handbook detailing the key information and as an on-going source of reference for the individual.

Induction must be timely, ensuring new staff obtain a comprehensive picture of the organization as early as possible. It is an on-going process, as staff have to be introduced to new environments as they are moved to different working areas or new job roles.

Training and development

Training and development aims to enhance the performance of staff, whether working at less than their best or working well, through changing their behaviour and attitudes in order to achieve the organization's objectives and targets. The goal should be to develop good working methods based on best practice and effective habits and skills, together with a better understanding of the purpose of the job and its contribution to business objectives and the standards of performance expected. This provides staff with a feeling of control over their work, increases their confidence and job satisfaction and helps to eliminate confusion, stress and fatigue.

A typical training programme for new room attendants is contained in Table 6.5.

Each training session requires careful planning with the purpose, objectives and outcomes clearly specified. The following aspects also need to be considered when designing the session:

- trainees – number, previous experience, culture, gender and age
- room layout and seating arrangements

Table 6.4 A typical stage 1 induction programme for housekeeping staff

Welcome and introductions	Team leaders, work colleagues
Administration	Completion of appointment forms, contracts, confidentiality/bribery forms, P45s
Essential places	Restaurant, toilet, locker areas, time clock, payroll
Conditions of service	Working week, rates of pay, period of notice, absences, sickness and holiday procedure, timekeeping, security, fire procedures, grievance and disciplinary procedure
Service operation information	Structure of the organization, who's who, business objectives and targets, role within the organization, liaison
Introduction to the job	Job description, hours of work, duty rotas, standards of quality, check levels of skills, check familiarity with equipment, plant and products, training arrangements
Health, safety and security	Health and safety arrangements, fire procedures, personal hygiene, legal implications, security awareness (only those aspects required at operational level if these areas are included in the divisional level induction)
Welfare arrangements	Protective clothing, occupational health, medicals, pension schemes, social clubs and activities
Remuneration	Rates of pay, allowances, payment arrangements
General tour	

Table 6.5 An example of the content of a training programme for a new room attendant

---

Room cleaning
Constituent tasks and how to undertake them:
- bed making, suction cleaning, damp dusting, ledges, paintwork, walls, telephones, bins and ashtrays, stains
- washing tea trays and pots
- replenishing room stocks, soft furnishings, bedding and bed linen
- checking of electrical items and lighting

Frequency of tasks
Standards to be achieved – appearance, hygiene, layout on completion
Time allowed for servicing the room
Bathroom cleaning
Constituent tasks and how to undertake them:
- cleaning bath, shower and curtain, basin, mirrors, bidet, toilet, floor, walls
- replenishing stocks

Frequency of tasks
Standards to be achieved
Time allowed for servicing the bathroom
Services (e.g. how to serve early morning tea)
Other issues
Laundry arrangements
Waste management
Care and use of equipment
Hygiene precautions and cross contamination
Health and safety
Fire and security
Interpersonal skills and attitudes to customers
Energy conservation

- content – level and breakdown into logical divisions for mastery
- introduction – impact to gain attention, put trainees at ease and motivate them
- variety of activities
- pace of learning
- practising of practical skills and correction of errors
- finale – recapping, summarizing, and testing understanding
- instructional techniques (e.g. demonstrations, discussions, role plays or simulations)
- handouts and visual aids
- duration.

Each session must be evaluated either through oral feedback or the use of questionnaires in order to effect improvements next time. Refresher training on key aspects will be needed over a period of time to update and reinforce the initial training.

Continuous professional development

This can be defined as 'the process of planned, continuing development of individuals throughout their career' (Institute of Management). Continuous professional development is becoming essential as careers are more likely to require a broadening of perceptions and knowledge or lateral moves, rather than a climb up the promotional ladder. The onus is now very firmly placed on the individual to take responsibility for the continuing assessment and satisfaction of his or her needs. In conjunction with this, many professional bodies are now expecting their members to professionally update themselves on a continuing basis. Indeed, some are legislating that members must produce evidence of a specified type or quantity of professional updating over an annual period. Individuals and organizations must respond to these demands.

Organizations will need to clarify their training and development strategy to accommodate continuous professional development and consider appropriate resource allocation. Continuous professional development will form an integral part of any appraisal or performance review procedure.

Evaluating the training and development

This is more than just measuring participant satisfaction, it is also about measuring the return on investment. Most organizations undertake the former as it is relatively simple to achieve. The latter is more problematic as the impact of training and development is difficult to measure and tends to be long term.

Evaluation is diagnostic and developmental in nature and is more pertinent when thought has been given to its purpose, the dimensions to be evaluated (see Table 6.6), the evaluation strategies to be used, who is to evaluate and give feedback and when and how often it should occur. Evaluation should aim to measure effectiveness of the training in terms of:

- participant satisfaction and plans for action
- an assessment of learning with regard to the amount of change in skills, knowledge and attitude
- application of the learning in the individual's workplace
- measurable business results from the application of learning (Kirkpatrick, 1997).

In the training and development context, evaluation is usually on-going, involving observations, discussions, reviews (e.g. of back injuries or labour turnover), surveys (e.g. customer satisfaction surveys) and questionnaires at appropriate times and at the end of the training. Individuals, line managers, trainers, training and development managers, the executive and, possibly, customers and suppliers can all have a key role to play in providing vital feedback.

Table 6.6 Some evaluation dimensions

Appropriateness, relevance and value of the training objectives and outcomes

Appropriateness, balance and variety of activities

Clarity of the aims, objectives, outcomes and instructions

Duration of the training

Effectiveness of the organization of the training

Relevance, sequencing, interest of the subject matter

Rigour, level and intellectually demanding nature of the training

Level and sufficiency of tutor support and feedback and manager support

Level and appropriateness of any assignments or assessments and the methods of assessment

Quality of the learning and development experience

Changes in and/or acquisition of attitudes, behaviour, skills and knowledge

Contribution of the training to achievement of the corporate mission, organizational objectives and culture and competitive advantage

Level to which training supports operational strategy

Competence of the trainers

Level to which training also reflects the needs of individuals

---

Training and development records

A comprehensive, up-to-date and accurate database of staff participating in training and development activities should be maintained. This helps to monitor attendance and identify staff who have been absent from training for some reason and who, therefore, still need training. Full costs associated with the training should also be recorded. Skills databases can also be useful.

Staff will no doubt require certificates of attendance and records of achievement for their learning portfolios. It is becoming more usual for staff to have a personal development plan agreed with their staff development or training officer and/or line manager as part of performance review. All parties will require a copy of this which must be updated on an on-going basis.

Training and development costs

The Investors in People standard encourages organizations to undertake a cost benefit analysis to quantify how much is being spent on training and to evaluate the benefits of the training and the value added in financial terms. It is often difficult to establish the true cost of training, particularly in terms of quantifying impromptu on the job training and the impact of training on the achievement of the business's objectives. The costs itemized in Table 6.7 need to be assessed.

Unfortunately, staff may leave during or after training and development and other organizations reap the benefits of the investment, but this should not eliminate the training effort.

National Vocational Qualifications (NVQs)

The origins of NVQs lie in the 'New Training Initiative' White Paper (MSC, 1981) which argued that there is a link between investment in training and development and commercial success, a perception deemed to be lacking in the UK at that time.

The National Council for Vocational Qualifications was established in 1986 to oversee the development of a new qualifications framework based on nationally agreed standards of performance, covering some 11 occupational areas. Lead bodies, which are occupationally focused organizations, were established with the specific objective of defining occupational standards and, thus, the NVQs based on them. Lead bodies undertake an occupational mapping exercise to provide a picture of the occupational area, its scope, boundaries and

Table 6.7 Training and development costs

Staffing costs	Trainer's salary or fees
	Wages of staff whilst training (including any overtime)
	Guest speaker's fees and expenses
	Planning and preparation time
	Technical help
Equipment costs	Audio-visual equipment purchasing or hire
	Computers
	Maintenance costs
Accommodation costs	Training room provision or room hire
	Overnight accommodation costs
	Loss of revenue potential if room is taken out of commission
Materials costs	Textbooks
	Learning packs, visual aids and other resource materials
	Stationery
Administrative costs	Clerical assistance
	Duplicating and printing
	Transport
Subsistence	Food and beverage costs

existing arrangements. Lead bodies then devise National Occupational Standards through a process known as functional analysis, which involves analysing the functions required for the competent performance of an occupational role. These standards form the basis of the NVQ. Organizations can adopt the occupational standards as standards of best practice without necessarily adopting the NVQ system.

Occupational Standards Councils have evolved to act as umbrella organizations to bring together existing lead bodies, professional bodies and others in similar or related sections in order to rationalize the number of lead bodies. NVQs are awarded through awarding bodies such as the City and Guilds of London Institute, Hotel Training Foundation, EDEXCEL (a new organization comprising BTEC and London Examinations) and the Management Verification Consortium. Existing professional bodies may incorporate lead body or awarding body roles – for example, the Hotel Training Foundation is the lead body arm of the Hotel and Catering Training Company.

All NVQs are positioned within a national framework of areas of occupational competence and levels of achievement ranging from NVQ level 1 to NVQ level 5 (see Table 6.8). The standards are grouped into units which constitute a discrete work activity. Each unit comprises a number of elements of competence. Performance is assessed against specified performance criteria or outcomes and across a range of contexts or situations within each element of competence.

The key features of NVQs are that they:

● are designed to accredit occupational competence (i.e. to measure and accredit an individual's ability to perform to the national standards in a particular occupational area), thus they are concerned with what people *do*
● have neither syllabus or curricula, but they do generally involve briefing sessions, action/self-development and assessment planning, progress review and some top up learning
● focus on the outcome of successful learning rather than the process or mode of learning and, as such, enable a range of different learning routes and opportunities to be made available to individuals
● are work-based qualifications judged on evidence produced by the candidate with much of the evidence required for assessment arising from the workplace
● require explicit evidence of knowledge and understanding to support assessment and learning
● are not graded – candidates are deemed 'competent' or 'not yet competent'

Table 6.8 NVQ level descriptors

Level	Descriptor
1	Competence which involves the application of knowledge in the performance of a range of varied work activities most of which may be routine or predictable
2	Competence which involves the application of knowledge in a significant range of varied work activities performed in a variety of contexts (some of the activities are complex and non-routine and there is some individual responsibility and autonomy) Collaboration with others perhaps through membership of a work group or team may often be a requirement
3	Competence which involves the application of knowledge in a broad range of varied work activities performed in a wide variety of contexts, most of which are complex and non-routine There is considerable responsibility and autonomy and control or guidance of others is often required
4	Competence which involves the application of knowledge in a broad range of complex technical and professional work activities performed in a wide variety of contexts and with a substantial degree of personal responsibility and autonomy Responsibility for the work of others and the allocation of resources is often present
5	Competence which involves the application of a significant range of fundamental principles across a wide and often unpredictable variety of contexts Very substantial personal autonomy and often significant responsibility for the work of others and for the allocation of substantial resources feature strongly as do personal accountabilities for analysis and diagnosis design planning execution and evaluation

(NVQ Criteria and Guidance, 1995: 11)

- can assist in improving business performance and results
- can introduce a targeted and systematic approach to training and development, resulting in a more economic use of resources to meet business objectives
- provide a possibility for crediting prior experiential learning
- open up access to assessment and qualification.

The basic NVQ process involves an individual:

- undertaking a self audit to compare his or her knowledge, experience and work activities with the appropriate occupational standards
- identifying gaps which need to be addressed through an individual development plan, which might include further training and/or undertaking other work activities or special work-based projects
- assembling evidence of competence usually in some kind of achievement log or learning portfolio
- assessment of competence either by direct observation of performance or other means (e.g. witness testimony or the learning portfolio).

NVQ assessment can be undertaken in house by qualified assessors from an approved assessment centre (e.g. a college or private training provider) or by a qualified in-house assessor. An organization can apply to the appropriate awarding body to become an approved assessment centre. Approval status is dependent on setting up the required infra-structure and quality assurance mechanisms.

National Education and Training Targets

These were launched in 1991 and are about raising standards and quality in education and training to enable the UK to compete more effectively in national, European and global markets. They are reviewed every so many years and are a way of:

- encouraging employers to invest in employees' development to achieve business success
- enabling all individuals to have access to education and training opportunities, leading to recognized qualifications which meet their needs and aspirations
- ensuring that all education and training develops self-reliance, flexibility and breadth in particular through fostering competence in key skills.

The targets are divided into foundation learning targets aimed at young people and lifetime learning targets aimed at the working population. The latter state that by the year 2000:

- 60 per cent of the workforce is to be qualified to NVQ level 3, Advanced GNVQ or 2 GCE A level standard
- 30 per cent of the workforce is to have vocational, professional, management or academic qualification at NVQ level 4 or above
- 70 per cent of all organizations employing 200 or more employees and 35 per cent of those employing 50 or more, will be recognized as Investors in People.

Mentoring

Mentoring often happens informally when an individual seeks advice and support from another individual. This may occur within or outside the organization. Often people do not recognize that they have a mentor. More and more organizations are introducing formal schemes to facilitate mentoring as a support mechanism. Mentoring can:

- identify potential more effectively
- induct staff more quickly

- improve the retention of staff
- encourage and support high flyers and ethnic and minority groups
- allow women to overcome the glass ceiling
- support self-development or work-based learning programmes
- include school children and students
- aid organizational change
- be used as a coping strategy, (e.g. when promoted to a new role).

Evidence suggests that as working patterns change, the significance of mentoring as a support mechanism will increase. As staff are given more autonomy, work on projects or increasingly in leaderless and/or multi-disciplinary teams, they become more isolated. Mentoring is useful as an individual coping strategy in this kind of scenario.

However mentoring is very complex with a variety of applications (as listed). It means different things to different people and the language of mentoring varies from one organization or discipline to another. It is important to have a shared understanding within an organization of what mentoring means. It is not easy to define, Megginson and Clutterbuck (1995, p. 13) do so succinctly in describing it as 'off line help by one person to another in making significant transitions in knowledge, work or thinking'.

Mentoring is a two-way process with the mentor developing as well as the mentee. As such, it is being used more widely by organizations as a personal development strategy. Benefits to the organization, mentor and mentee are identified in Table 6.9.

Mentoring is a process with four definable stages, namely an orientation and getting started stage, a period of adolescence followed by a maturing period and, finally, termination. Both mentor and mentee need to understand this process and the learning cycle (see Figure 6.1) which is at the heart of the mentoring process in order to maximize the experience. Research

...tional	Mentor	Mentee/Learner
Widening of skills base and competencies in line with the organizations strategic goals	Realizes and addresses own learning gaps	Develops learning, analytical and reflective skills
Alternative to external training	Learns to give and take criticism	Develops organizational and professional knowledge
More cost-effective personal development programme	Develops organizational and professional knowledge	Develops political awareness
Develops habits of trust and confidentiality	Keeps up-to-date	Develops own practice
Gives senior management a more informed view of the organization's talent	Networks	Learns to take risks
	Improves leadership, organizational and communication skills	Learns to accept criticism
Use for succession planning	Learns to challenge, stimulate and reflect	Supported through transition
Helps achieve mission/vision	Develops higher profile within organizations	Possible accelerated professional development
Develops a mature management population	Feels good and increases job satisfaction	Develops autonomy and independence
	Passes on knowledge and experience	Increases in maturity
	Improves teamwork and cooperation	Increases in confidence
	Provides stimulation	Broadens horizons
	Gives competitive edge	

has shown that training and briefing are essential for both ﬢ
ties participating in a formal scheme. A mentoring scheme is
more likely to be successful if the following criteria have been
considered:

- the reasons for and aims of the scheme
- if mentoring is consonant with the organization's structure
  and values
- who will run the scheme
- who the mentors will be and how they will be selected
- who will be mentored, why and how they will be selected
- how mentors and mentees will be matched and paired
- what resources are required and available
- what briefing and training will be given to both parties
- how mentors will be supported and if they will be rewarded
  in some way
- when, how and by whom the scheme will be monitored
  and evaluated.

Caring for your staff

Welfare of staff has always been an important issue, but never
more so than in today's climate when staff can feel insecure,
threatened, vulnerable and isolated. The level of support which
an organization gives to its staff and the extent to which it is
concerned with their physical and emotional needs will be
reflected in its level of staff turnover, sickness and absenteeism and retention rates, and in the achievement of quality
standards, customer care and customer satisfaction. A staff
welfare and care policy can encourage staff identification with
the organization and, thus, encourage loyalty and improve
morale. It is also a valuable way of communicating the ethos,
values and management style of the organization to staff.
Indeed, it can be perceived as a competitive advantage.

Such a welfare and care policy embraces the provision of:

- facilities for:
  - residential and non-residential staff
  - social, leisure and sporting activities
  - occupational health and medical care
  - safe, comfortable and secure working environments
  - personal hygiene
  - breaks, meals, snacks and refreshments
- support mechanisms, including:
  - training and development, particularly in health and safety
  - counselling
  - harassment support
  - equal opportunities.

Good conditions of service, including pay rates, sickness and holiday entitlements and pension schemes are also important features of a staff welfare and care policy.

The cost of welfare and care provision must be viewed in terms of reducing labour turnover, easing recruitment, reducing absenteeism, improving retention of staff and developing a well-motivated and stable workforce with high morale.

References and further reading

Association of Graduate Recruiters (1995) *Skills for Graduates in the 21st Century*.

Blanchard, K., Carew, D. and Parisi-Carew, E. (1996) *The One Minute Manager – Building High Performance Teams*. Harper Collins Business.

Boutall, T. (1995) *The Good Manager's Guide*. MCI.

Harvey-Jones (1995) in Consenting Adults – Making the Most of Mentoring, Channel 4 Television.

DES (1981) *White Paper: Education and Training for the 21st Century (England and Wales)*.

Institute of Management Continuing Professional Development *The IM Guide*.

Kirkpatrick, D. (1997) In (J. Matchett, ed.) *Management Skills and Development – Strategies and Initiative in Training and Development*.

Lloyd, B. (1996) Corridors of responsibility lead to long term success. *Professional Manager*, March, 7.

MCI Effective Manager (1993) *Module 9: Everyone's a Customer*.

Megginson, D. and Clutterbuck, D. (1995) *Mentoring in Action – A Practical Guide for Managers*. Kogan Page.

MSC (1981) A New Training Initiative: Agenda for action, Manpower Services Commission.

NCVQ (1995) *NVQ Criteria and Guidance*.

Pedler, M., Burgoyne, J. and Boydell, T. (1997) *The Learning Company – A Strategy for Substantive Development* (2nd edn). McGraw-Hill, Publishing Co.

Swieringa, J. and Wierdsman, A. (1992) *Becoming a Learning Organisation – Beyond the Learning Curve*. Addison-Wesley Publishing Co.

7
Monitoring and controlling service provision

Aims and objectives

This chapter aims to:

- introduce the concepts of monitoring and quality control
- analyse the nature of monitoring in a service operation
- define the purpose of monitoring, the importance of the monitoring specification and the elements of a monitoring system
- define quality assessment standards and methods of assessing and measuring quality
- emphasize the need for and preparation of expenditure and sales budgets
- consider the role of financial control, particularly variance analysis
- identify useful performance indicators.

Monitoring and quality control

Monitoring is a form of quality control. It is a continuous process which provides a means of:

- ensuring that the product or service has been delivered
- ensuring that the standard of product or service delivery complies with the quality standards set in the service

specification or service level agreement and delivery specification

- identifying and assessing the actual performance
- detecting unsatisfactory performance and incomplete work
- detecting work performed to a standard higher than the minimum acceptable level specified
- supporting payments to be made to contractors and making deductions from payments in the case of non-conformance
- identifying recurring problems or difficulties
- reviewing the service specification in order to make amendments where necessary to achieve improvements in the service, reduce standards which are too high and, if possible, reduce costs.

One of its main aims is to report to both executive and operations management on the quality of the service being provided. Service operations management can then take action to ensure that a satisfactory and cost-effective service is being provided.

However, quality control tends to focus on poor quality and on finding errors and correcting them rather than on improving the whole system to eliminate mistakes at source. It means that a non-conforming product or service must have been produced before corrective action can be taken. Non-conformance incurs inefficiency, waste and expense.

Quality control procedures include:

- controlling key input resources to ensure that only components and items conforming to specification are accepted from suppliers
- controlling processes to ensure that production and service delivery conforms to the agreed specification
- inspecting, sampling and product testing to ensure that only products and service elements that conform to specification reach the customers
- collecting feedback from customers and other stakeholders over specified periods to ascertain whether standards of quality are being achieved consistently and control and

inspection procedures are effective (Henley Distance Learning Ltd, 1991).

The nature of monitoring in a facilities service operation

Facilities services, particularly those involving intangible service elements, (e.g. courtesy or helpfulness), rely heavily on individual staff to achieve the required output. Training is, therefore, imperative in this context. Intangible service elements are very difficult to define precisely and so are difficult to measure objectively and quantitatively. Thus, in these circumstances, reliance has to be placed on qualitative measures and subjective judgement.

In a manufacturing situation, where a physical component can be produced to a precisely defined specification, it is much easier to apply the concept of monitoring quality. On production, the component can be tested against specification by using accurate and objective measurement techniques (Grant Thornton, 1987).

In service situations, there is no reliable means for testing quality other than personal observation and subjective judgement. Monitoring of quality is further complicated by the time difference between production, service and monitoring. For example, the production of a meal is a tangible product and elements of it (e.g. temperature) can be accurately measured. However, the temperature could comply to the quality standard set when tested in the kitchen, but the meal could be cold by the time it is served in the restaurant. In this situation, at least two different sections of the organization are responsible for the delivery of the service package. This introduces a futher difficulty in terms of identifying who is responsible for the problem as it is perceived by the customer.

In the case of the cleaning service, first it is very difficult to define what 'clean' means and second there is no scientific way to measure whether a whole area is clean. Thus, measurement in this context becomes very subjective – relying on observation and personal comment. Although a room may be cleaned efficiently and according to the prescribed procedure, during the time which elapses between cleaning and monitoring it could have received very heavy usage or have been abused by particularly untidy and dirty users.

The monitoring specification

The monitoring system should be designed in conjunction with the service specification or service level agreement. The monitoring process consists of reviewing the service being provided, collecting data about its performance and recording major problems identified by the users.

The monitoring specification, whether for in house or external contract purposes, comprises:

● the purpose of monitoring
● the standards of quality
● the scope of the monitoring system
● the specifications for quality assessment
● quality assessment and measurement
● the frequency of assessment
● coordination of the monitoring process and provision of feedback
● remedial action
● documentation of feedback and production of reports
● the use of external contractor's quality procedures
● a system review.

The monitoring specification should be documented in the form of a monitoring manual, for example, to:

● ensure understanding of the monitoring process by all stakeholders
● ensure continuity of the monitoring role

- aid training of subsequent monitors
- enable the monitoring system to be reviewed
- provide the official documentation of the description of the monitoring system, its scope and the standards of quality defined.

Defining standards of quality

In order to accomplish the aims of the monitoring process, it is necessary to define what standard of quality is required and how it is to be measured. Generally speaking, standards of quality are defined either by outcome or process or in qualitative or quantitative terms. For example, the following example defines the standard for bath cleaning by outcome or end result. When the bath has been cleaned there should be:

- no hairs in the plug hole
- no discernible grease line
- no waterspots on the tap
- no traces of cleaning agent
- a dry internal surface
- shiny taps
- plug chain hung over the tap
- new soap in the soap tray
- a clean bath mat over the side.

Where activities cannot be defined precisely, standards are defined in qualitative terms such as 'clean', 'satisfactory' or 'neatly folded'. Such definitions are open to individual interpretation, thus making measurement difficult and variable from one monitor to another. In this case, it may be useful to define the processes which must be undertaken to achieve the required end product. For example, on a daily basis the floor surface must be:

- swept with a mop sweeper
- damp mopped using neutral detergent.

Where it is possible to use precise measurements, standards may be defined in quantitative terms, for example:

- dirty linen will be collected at 14.00 hours plus or minus 30 minutes
- top sheets will be returned in bundles of 20
- the final wash temperature for flame retardant items should not exceed 75°C.

Defining the scope of the monitoring system

This involves first identifying the main activities specified in the service specification which have to be undertaken and consequently monitored. These activities might include single tasks (e.g. laying the table or storage of wine) or groups of activities (e.g. processing bed linen or performing a series of cleaning tasks). In the cleaning context, it may be more appropriate to select a physical area or area type (e.g. a bedroom or public area) as a suitable basis for monitoring.

The next step is to determine the specific dimensions or aspects of each activity or physical area which have to be monitored in order to determine whether each activity or area has been undertaken to the required standard. For example, in the case of storage of wine, the specific aspects selected for monitoring could include receiving the wine, wine storage controls, wine issuing procedures and wine storage temperature. In the case of cleaning, a physical location such as an hotel bedroom with en-suite bathroom, the following aspects for monitoring would be selected.

- Bedroom – bed making, floor cleaning and furniture cleaning.
- Bathroom – sanitary fitting cleaning, floor cleaning and supply of new provisions.

It may be possible and/or preferable to breakdown these aspects even further, for example, into the specific tasks of suction cleaning, damp mopping and damp dusting or into specific items of furniture and fittings (e.g. baths, basins or showers) to be assessed. There will also be a number of general aspects to monitor including hygiene, health and safety, security and equipment usage and maintenance.

It is useful to grade these activities or physical locations according to their importance. For example, the monitoring dimensions could be graded according to their contribution to the quality service provision such as primary aspects which are 'fundamental to the service and where failure would be regarded as serious breakdown to the service' and which have significant cost implications and secondary aspects which are not critical to service delivery or cost. Secondary aspects might not be monitored or be monitored only infrequently where cost and size of the total monitoring operation are issues. The physical location may be graded according to the degree of risk, usage or in an hotel prestige, so that a higher level of monitoring can be applied to a higher risk or usage or more prestigious area. Grading could be as follows:

- high hygiene risk areas (e.g. kitchens, sanitary areas and swimming pools)
- low hygiene risk areas (e.g. guest bedrooms)
- no hygiene risk areas(e.g. offices and public areas).

Alternatively, the main entrance could be classed as high usage and a store as low usage or highly priced suites as high prestige areas and the staff refectory as a high usage but low prestige area. The grading will affect the frequency of monitoring (see page 207).

Quality assessment specifications

The next stage is to develop a specification against which to assess the quality of each dimension, activity or physical location identified. Two examples of quality assessment specifications are presented in Tables 7.1 and 7.2. Table 7.1 contains an example of a quality assessment specification for an activity and Table 7.2 a specification for a physical location. Each example contains:

- a statement of the overall standard required
- the particular aspects or dimensions to be monitored
- the standard of quality expected
- the method of assessment to be used
- the frequency of assessment
- the person who will assess.

The standard defined will be based on 'normal' circumstances. However, sometimes unexpected or abnormal circumstances (e.g. inclement weather or vandalism) could have occurred which could affect the method used and the result achieved. The monitoring must be flexible enough to cope with such deviations. Quality standards must be amended when necessary, particularly if any changes are made to the service specification. The defined standards of quality and assessment specifications must be communicated to staff through training and team briefing. It is unfair to expect staff to know the quality to be achieved, or worse still to discipline them for achieving poor results, if they have never been informed of it.

Assessing and measuring quality

A variety of methods can be used to assess quality in different circumstances. Quantitative assessment can be used where it is possible to measure precisely. Hygiene and health and safety assessment, for example, in a patient hotel situation might include:

- bacterial counts in high risk areas, where clinical standards are required, and in food and food preparation areas
- air counts to determine bacterial levels in the atmosphere

Table 7.1 Quality assessment specification for a physical area

Location: En-suite bathroom in the presidential suite
Grade: Hygienically clean, prestigious area
Service standard: The area will be cleaned to a standard which is hygienically clean to minimize the risk of cross-infection, ensure comfort, eliminate frustration and represent value for money

Monitoring aspects	Standard of quality	Method of assessment	Frequency	Responsibility for assessment
Primary				
Floor covering	No stains, scuffs, litter, dust or	Visual check, no exceptions allowed	daily	Room assistant Assistant Housekeeper
	spillages	Visual check,	daily	Room assistant
	Complete coverage No polish build up	mobile items moved, no exceptions allowed		Assistant Housekeeper
Wash basins/ splash backs	No smears or stains	Visual check, no exceptions allowed	daily	Room assistant Assistant Housekeeper
	No hairs in plug hole Taps buffed			
	Overflow	Visual check	weekly	Assistant Housekeeper
Waste bin	Correct colour coded bag inserted Changed daily	Visual check, no exceptions	daily	Assistant Housekeeper
Secondary				
None				

(Adapted from Grant Thornton, 1987)

Table 7.2 Quality assessment specification for an activity

Activity:	Collection and delivery of linen to central area
Grade:	All aspects graded as primary
Service standard:	Collections and deliveries to be made at the times detailed in the specification, using the specified equipment and procedures
Location:	Loading bay and holding area

Monitoring aspects	Standard of quality	Method of assessment	Frequency
Adherence to times of collection and delivery	Delivery times as scheduled (plus or minus 30 minutes)	Actual time of receipt/ collection as noted on goods notes	Daily and weekly
Correct containers used	Conformity to standard at all times	Number of examples found in unacceptable condition	Daily and weekly
Correct bagging of outbound items	Conformity to standard at all times	Number of examples found in unacceptable condition	Daily and weekly
Correct outer covering	According to agreed procedure between contractor and facilities manager	Number of examples found in unacceptable condition	Daily and weekly
Correct location and storage of full and empty containers (e.g. under cover)	Following specified procedure and operating rules for loading bay activities	Acceptable/ unacceptable instances	Daily and weekly

(Adapted from Grant Thornton, 1987)

- swab tests on equipment, in cleaning water, in dishwashers, in laundry equipment, in toilets and on shower heads to assess numbers and types of micro-organisms present

● use of a slit sampler to evaluate the effect on air disturbance caused by equipment such as suction cleaners or mops or brushes.

Other examples of measurement could include:

● physical stock checks
● temperature measurement of food, ovens, dishwashers and laundry equipment
● weighing of food waste
● checking of specified times at which activities are expected to happen.

Qualitative assessment includes visual inspections of the outcome of an activity or series of activities (e.g. assessing the standard of finish of the laundering, ironing and folding of linen, the standard of cleanliness achieved in a physical area or the cleanliness and state of equipment after use). Observation of performance and working methods is another form of qualitative assessment used when specific methods have been defined within the quality standard or specification and particularly to check compliance with hygiene and health and safety procedures. Observation is time consuming and, in reality, it is probably the end result which is checked rather than the process. It is not possible to visually inspect everything and, therefore, often sampling is undertaken (see page 207).

In some circumstances, it might be appropriate to develop and use point-scoring assessment methods. For example, in a cleaning situation it is possible to allocate a number of points to each task according to its importance, degree of risk and type of location. A failure limit is set for each area above which the overall standard will be considered unacceptable. The higher the degree of risk, the lower the acceptable fault level. The number and types of areas failing can be compared against the total number of areas and the contract/tender budget. An alternative approach is to assign a number of points to a task depending on the time-value allocated and its importance. If the task has not been adequately performed, the assigned number of points are recorded as a penalty. The total number of penalty points can be expressed as a percentage of the total available points for all tasks in that physical area. A specified number of areas will be sampled over a period of time (e.g. a week or a month). This information can then be used to produce a general statement of performance and to calculate financial deductions for non-compliance, from payments to contractors.

All assessment methods selected must be capable of being repeated consistently by different monitors.

Frequency of assessment

This will be determined to some extent by the frequency of performance of tasks and activities as specified in the service and/or delivery specifications, the degree of risk and the type of area. Too frequent assessment will be time consuming and, thus, costly and there may in fact be no appreciable change in the observable results since the last inspection or test. The monitoring system must encompass the assessment of periodic activities and the reassessment of activities which have had to be rectified. This requires the design of a good information system.

In reality, it is not financially viable or practicable to inspect all products, areas and processes every time they are undertaken. Assessment is time consuming and generates large amounts of information to be collated, sorted, documented and stored. However, assessment must be regular, unpredictable and valid to be of value. Therefore, sampling of a limited number of tasks or areas – using a variety of techniques – is usually applied.

Random sampling, which involves simply selecting tasks to be assessed at random, is difficult to apply because the process can be biased. Stratified sampling involves sampling 'one of each type' (e.g. one sleeping area and one sanitary area), whereas multi-stage sampling involves dividing the activities into groups (e.g. physical areas: bathrooms and public areas) and then selecting a few of each group to sample. Quota sampling is non-random and involves defining a quota of, for example, each type of physical area to be sampled. Quotas can be adjusted to accommodate more higher graded areas or more frequent assessment. A number of computerized monitoring software packages are now available which select the activities or areas to be assessed within the parameters set by the software user.

Who monitors?

The monitor's role is to ensure that a service which matches customer requirements is provided to all users. Ideally, the monitor has no line responsibility for any of the services, but is simply providing monitoring feedback on which the facilities manager and individual services managers can take action. In a large organization, particularly where total outsourcing has occurred, it may be deemed necessary to employ an independent monitor. However, this contributes another expense and a potential problem centres around whether one individual has the background, experience and ability to monitor such diverse services encountered within the facilities management context or whether someone should be appointed for each service. Monitors must be professionally competent to make decisions which could cause variations to be made to the service specification or affect the payment of an external service provider. Individuals will bring their own values, perceptions and bias into the process and steps must be taken to ensure that misconceptions do not occur and results are not distorted. In large organizations, it may be necessary to have a team of monitors – particularly when a number of sites have to be assessed. In small operations, the facilities manager or designated representative(s) will assume the monitoring role. However, duality of role can lead to tensions unless both management/supervisory and monitoring roles are defined and recognized.

In addition, a number of different people could be involved in assessment and feedback. Each dimension, activity or physical location identified for assessment must be allocated to a particular person. Those involved in assessing standards of quality and performance could include service users or customers (both internal and external) (see 'Measuring customer satisfaction'), clients in the contract situation, departmental heads, all facilities services managers and technical specialists (e.g. microbiologists, pest control officers, control of infection officers, fire officers, health and safety inspectors, Investors in People and ISO 9000 inspectors). However, a balance between feedback from service users and customers and sampling by monitors or team leaders should be sought. Those involved must be fully conversant with the service and delivery specifications, the quality standards and the assessment methods to be used and, where applicable, the terms and conditions of the contract. They must also know how to record, collate and present their results, to whom they will present the results and when.

It is not unusual in some organizations for individuals to review their own performance and inspect the outcome of their own efforts with a view to rectifying problems quickly and encouraging continuous improvement. Peer monitoring is another approach which involves feedback from work or team colleagues.

Checklists

It is usual to design checklists or report formats for use by those involved in the monitoring process to ensure feedback is received on the dimensions required and to encourage consistency and a systematic approach. A checklist is only useful when it is well designed, covers all the essential dimensions to be assessed, allows sufficient space for comment, is simple and easy to complete. It should focus attention and aid concentration. The format should allow for the time and date of the assessment to be recorded and the signature of the monitor. In some cases, it might be appropriate for the assessment to be verified by the head of department. Work schedules will help monitors know what activities are happening and at what time.

Attention to detail can make the difference between a high standard and a mediocre standard being achieved. In the cleaning context, inspection of the less obvious places (e.g. under and behind doors, backs of wardrobe tops, under basins, behind toilet pedestals or in corners) should be undertaken.

Remedial action for unsatisfactory work

Good work and the attainment of the required standard should be given credit and praise. Consistent attainment of high standards could provide the basis for a reward or incentive scheme.

When performance and standards achieved are unsatisfactory, work should be rectified and subsequently re-inspected. In the in-house situation, deficiencies should be rectified as soon as possible with the person concerned preferably before he or she goes off duty. Different actions will be taken, depending on the problem encountered. Within the cleaning context, a task may have to be undertaken if it has been missed or repeated if it has not been undertaken to a satisfactory standard. A whole area may even have to be recleaned. On the other hand, it may be more appropriate to undertake the task in the next cleaning process. Repetitive failure needs to be investigated. In addition, equipment might need to be serviced, retraining or refresher training might be needed or disciplinary action may even be required.

In a contract situation, the contractor will be informed of the unsatisfactory results and given a period of time, as specified in the contract, in which to rectify the problem. Further inspection will then be necessary to ensure that the problem has been rectified. Financial penalties for failure to comply with the specification could be incurred by the contractor under these circumstances.

Documentation and reporting

Outcomes of the monitoring process will have to be collated, summarized and analysed for presentation to senior facilities and executive management and possibly also to clients or customers at specified intervals. Management will need to decide what information it requires, for what purposes, in what format and how often. All resulting courses of action and changes to procedures, standards or even the service or delivery specification must be documented and communicated to the appropriate people.

Making use of external contractors quality procedures

It is beneficial in a contract situation to incorporate the contractor's own quality control and assurance procedures into the monitoring system. This should reduce costs and eliminate duplication. However, it is only viable if it produces reliable results and is more cost effective. Initially, it will involve a review of the contractor's quality procedures to determine how reliable they are. Any weaknesses or gaps should be identified and these should be reappraised periodically as part of the on-going monitoring system. Good communication and regular meetings with contractors are imperative.

Review of the monitoring system

The monitoring system itself will have to be kept under constant scrutiny to ensure that it consistently achieves its aims and the monitoring workload does not become too great in comparison to the outcomes achieved. The cost of the monitoring system must be commensurate with the consistent achievement of customer satisfaction and reduction of mistakes and 'non-quality' experiences.

Computerized monitoring

Some software packages are now available for monitoring. In the cleaning context, these are based around the use of hand-held computer units allowing immediate monitoring feedback to be input into area-specific checklists. In some cases, there is only need to enter specific comments against the areas where problems have been identified. Non-conformance can be tracked and analysis undertaken by location, team or operative. Some packages enable area or activity samples to be selected according to parameters defined by the software user.

Financial monitoring of performance

Performance and achievements can also be monitored by means of financial control processes, including variance analysis and comparison of a variety of performance indicators.

Budgetary control

Financial control begins with the preparation of the budget, which can be defined as an expression in financial terms of an intention to follow a specific course of action within a defined period of time and in the short term. The terms 'budget' and 'estimates' are often used synonymously, but here estimates are defined as plans developed within broad financial targets to project two to three years ahead. Forecasts are looking five to ten years ahead and are even less accurate projections of future plans.

Benefits of budgets

Financial monitoring involves scrutininzing the planned expenditure and reviewing the utilization of the resources devoted to these actions. More specifically, budgets are beneficial as they:

- help to determine total costs, costs per cost centre and unit costs
- aid price determination
- enable comparisons, including actual expenditure against budgeted expenditure, and benchmarking to be undertaken
- contribute to assessing performance and measuring effectiveness
- bring inefficiencies to light
- improve future planning and forecasting
- help to achieve better allocation of resources
- help to establish the 'best' level of activity
- provide a framework for change
- forewarn of cash difficulties
- contribute to strategic planning by helping to define and prioritize objectives.

Budget preparation

Annual budgets will need to be prepared for each of the facilities services probably three to six months in advance. When approved and amalgamated, these will constitute the master budget for the whole facilities service operation. The budget preparation cycle is outlined in Figure 7.1. Budgets are an effective means of communication, particularly when staff teams are involved in their preparation and monitoring. This is often

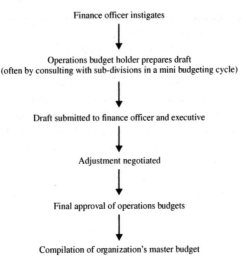

Finance officer instigates

Operations budget holder prepares draft
(often by consulting with sub-divisions in a mini budgeting cycle)

Draft submitted to finance officer and executive

Adjustment negotiated

Final approval of operations budgets

Compilation of organization's master budget

Figure 7.1 Budget preparation cycle.

referred to as 'bottom up' budgeting and involves teams analysing the cost implications of their work, negotiating their draft
budget with their manager and justifying their financial plans.
The proposed budget may not be accepted in its entirety, so
adjustments will have to be made. Consequently, managers
will have to operate within tighter financial constraints,
particularly in today's climate when all areas are having to
make efficiency gains. The individual budgets for each operation are then consolidated to form the master budget for the
whole organization.

Budgets may be prepared on the basis of performance in
previous years (referred to as 'incremental budgeting') or from
scratch (referred to as 'zero based budgeting'). The former
method is easier and quicker than the latter, but can repeat
errors and lead to unnecessary spending. The latter is time
consuming (MCI, 1993). Budget preparation requires historical information, knowledge about the future and knowledge
of organizational guidelines. Historical information includes

actual expenditure and budgets from previous years and past trends and performance statistics. Future knowledge includes new plans and policies, proposed changes in wage agreements, for example, financial and sales estimates for the next few years and forthcoming strategic objectives.

Organizational guidelines will provide information on capital charging and allocation of overheads, carry-over of surplus finance from one financial year to the next and the extent to which finance can be vired between cost centres. The style of budget presentation will vary according to the organization's financial structure and procedures, but a standard format is beneficial.

Expenditure budgets

A cost centre is the heading for the smallest accounting unit to which costs can be allocated. It may be a physical location or an activity. Cost centres will vary from one budget or organization to another. Within the facilities management context, cleaning, maintenance and catering may each constitute a cost centre within the overall facilities budget and as such have their own budget broken down into further cost centres. Typical cost centres within a facilities services budget would be:

- labour (including total costs for each grade of staff employed, plus enhanced rate costs, overtime – if appropriate – and bonus costs); these figures will be calculated from the establishment figure, deployment schedules and duty rotas
- supplies and materials (including cleaning agents, cleaning equipment, depreciation of equipment or replacement costs, guest supplies, stationery, crockery, workwear and food supplies); historic data and store records are useful when estimating these costs
- linen and laundry (including soft furnishings, repairs,

laundering, dry cleaning and replacement costs); where there is an on-site laundry, laundry equipment and agents would also be included and, again historic, stores and processing records are used in estimating these costs

- maintenance (including external maintenance of grounds, gardens and external fabric and internal maintenance of surfaces, structures, plant and equipment and redecoration costs)
- contract services (including cleaning, window cleaning, floral decorations, catering, linen hire, pest control, equipment maintenance and security); these costs are relatively easy to estimate from historical data and usage projections
- training and staff development (see Table 6.7)
- workwear (including the cost of uniforms and protective clothing issued to all grades of staff and, in some circumstances, their laundry and dry cleaning costs too)
- furniture and furnishings (including all types of furniture, carpets, curtains, blankets and bedspread replacements).

Some of these costs will be fixed and some will be variable, depending on the fluctuations in the workload. Items which are not within the scope of the facilities management remit should not be included in the budget. In addition to operational costs, service costs (e.g. administration, sales, advertising and marketing), heating, lighting and power, telephone charges and any other items which cannot be allocated to any other budget must be calculated and apportioned according to company policy.

In the standard system of hotel accounts, repairs and maintenance, plant and machinery and property cost centres are not included in calculating hotel operating profit in order that income, expenditure and profit can be compared more easily throughout the industry. However, property is the major capital asset and in the hotel context, is the core business and, as such, should not be ignored. It possesses an intrinsic property value which can be increased and will certainly diminish if not maintained or managed effectively. In some organizations, capital charging occurs, whereby a pre-determined proportion of the property cost and overheads (e.g. energy) are charged back to the operational areas according to space and facilities utilization. It is also worth considering the opportunity costs of the property in terms of whether a higher return on the investment could be accrued from an alternative use of the whole or part of the building or site or even whether it is more beneficial to sell the property.

Financial monitoring and variance analysis

To facilitate financial monitoring, 'cost statements' or 'operating statements' are produced at certain fixed intervals (e.g. weekly, monthly or on a daily basis if 'on line'). These statements enable actual performance to be measured and compared with the budgetary figure. Variances between these two figures which may be over or under budget can then be investigated and possible causes identified. Variances may be related to changes in policies, costs, prices, timing, usage or some unforeseen circumstances (e.g. a long period of cold weather or a water shortage). There are two possible courses of action. Action can be taken to bring performance back to budget and to use resources more efficiently or the budget can be adjusted perhaps by viring expenditure from one budget head to another. It will be necessary to consider if better control could have been taken to prevent the problem or if the variance was a one-off or a long-term change. From time to time, the budget itself should be evaluated to determine if it is:

● still reflecting the key strategic objectives
● flexible enough to support organizational change
● providing timely information which is appropriate to the management's requirements

- revealing operating problems, inefficiencies, long-term trends and opportunities to reduce costs
- identifying quality costs and problems
- identifying ways of improving the performance of the operation.

Capital budgets

Capital projects require the development of a discrete budget to demonstrate the existence of a coordinated plan and to justify the expenditure on a particular project. Projects need to be prioritized where several projects are competing for available funding. This budget is subsequently used to monitor and control progress and achievement of the project.

Income or sales budgets

Managers responsible for a sales function, often referred to as a 'cost and profit centre', or income generation will need to prepare a sales or income budget. This budget is the key to profit planning and resource allocation to achieve sales targets. The planned level of sales will affect the operating budget as well as the cash-flow situation.

Preparation of this budget will involve analysing the previous year's sales to determine any trends and circumstances which affected overall achievement of targets. The level of sales for the forthcoming year will have to be forecast, bearing in mind knowledge of past trends, prevailing business and market conditions, local circumstances, pricing considerations, expected growth rates, marketing efforts and availability of facilities, services and labour. Financial implications and different scenarios can be evaluated using computerized spreadsheets, but a realistic sales budget must result which sets achievable sales targets.

To facilitate the monitoring of sales and income or revenue

generated, sales reports are also produced at pre-determined fixed intervals (e.g. daily or weekly). Sales reports normally include a sales summary from each sales outlet or defined profit centre, including rooms, restaurants, bars and leisure outlets in an hotel context. The sales summary will identify individual customer transactions attributable to each sales outlet, the total revenue received in that area and the total business undertaken in statistical terms using appropriate performance indicators and unit costs for comparative purposes. All sales attributable to individual customers and often to the defined market segments will be summarized.

Performance indicators

It is usual to monitor various aspects of performance and achievements using specified performance indicators and to compare them against the budget and against past performance, for example, yesterday, the same day last week, last month or the same period last year. Plotting of these figures on an on-going basis helps to determine trends, peaks and troughs in business and performance. It also provides invaluable information for forecasting purposes.

Within the hotel context, as profitability is essentially reliant on the maximization of daily revenue from room sales it is usual to analyse both occupancy and revenue performance. A range of occupancy statistics as identified in Table 7.3 are normally compared, all of which are of value but taken in isolation do not necessarily reflect an accurate picture. In order to calculate these statistics, it is essential to clarify:

- the total number of rooms available
- the variety of room types and the number of each
- the flexibility of the rooms for alternative uses
- the number of fold-away beds which can be accommodated at peak periods.

Table 7.3 Occupancy statistics

Type and calculation	Uses	Limitations
Room occupancy $\dfrac{\textit{number of rooms sold} \times 100}{\text{total number of rooms 1}}$	Indicates percentage of rooms sold	Does not reflect: • number of occupants • rooms unavailable
Available room occupancy $\dfrac{\textit{number of rooms sold} \times 100}{\text{number of rooms 1 available for letting}}$	Reflects number of rooms available for letting, out of order, being refurbished, etc.	Does not reflect number of occupants
Bed occupancy $\dfrac{\textit{number of beds sold} \times 100}{\text{total possible beds 1}}$	Indicates number of beds occupied rather than rooms	Does not reflect: • double occupancy of double beds • rooms unavailable
Sleeper occupancy $\dfrac{\textit{number of sleepers} \times 100}{\text{total possible sleepers 1}}$	Indicates number of occupants Can compare room versus sleeper occupancy	Does not reflect rooms unavailable
Income occupancy $\dfrac{\textit{actual accommodation income}}{\text{number of rooms sold}}$	Reflects discounts and complimentary rooms Reflects strategy of doubles sold to single occupants Indicates the percentage of potential income lost on a particular night	Does not reflect number of occupants

It is not sufficient to aim purely for capacity occupancy, revenue also needs to be maximized. Thus, it is essential to calculate capacity occupancy at full rack rate, including income which can be generated through the use of fold-away beds.

This helps managers to compare revenue generated with the full potential revenue, determine the extent of lost revenue and investigate reasons for this. It is useful to also determine the potential revenue at full rack rate but with only single occupancy and the occupancy percentage required to break even and cover fixed and variable costs.

The actual revenue achieved will reflect price variations (e.g. discounts, special terms and complimentary accommodation allocated). The average room rate is most commonly used to measure the standard of room sales:

$$\text{Average room rate} = \frac{\text{accommodation income}}{\text{number of rooms sold}}$$

An increase in the average room rate achieved reflects maximization of double occupancy or proportionally higher number of more expensive rooms sold. A decrease reflects selling rooms at less than rack rate or single occupancy. By plotting all sales and calculating the standard deviation, it can be determined whether most room prices have been variable or whether most rooms were sold around the average room rate. It is also useful for comparative purposes to calculate the potential average room rate, that is the average room rate that could be achieved if all the occupied rooms were sold at full rack rate and no discounting had occurred. The rate spread which is the difference between the potential average room rates at double occupancy and single occupancy denotes the maximum and minimum average room rate. The average sleeper or guest rate can also be calculated.

Room rates are subject to great variations in selling price according to the type and convenience of the room, room occupancy, the season and demand, and a range of discounts are offered to different market segments at different times of the year. It is beneficial to monitor the impact of pricing and discounting decisions on revenue achieved. This can be done using a discounting grid which will show the equivalent occupancy which must be achieved in order to maintain the desired pre-determined room revenue level as the amount of discounting is increased or decreased.

$$\text{Equivalent occupancy} = \text{current occupancy} \times \frac{\text{rack rate} - \text{marginal cost}}{\text{rack rate} \times 1 - \text{discount \%}) - \text{marginal cost}.}$$

The marginal cost (defined as the cost of producing another unit) is really the operational cost in this case of producing a room. It includes the costs of stationery, giveaways, beverages, cleaning (labour and agents), soap, toiletries and the processing of bed linen. It is negligible when compared to the room price as it does not cover a proportion of all the costs involved in providing the whole facility (e.g. rent, rates, cleaning, maintenance and heating of public areas, telephone and rental costs).

In addition, it is possible to determine what is a reasonable level of potential revenue for a combination of different levels of occupancy at different rates (Lovelock, 1984). This involves calculating the average unit price efficiency rate, which is the average room rate as a percentage of the rack rate. For example, if the average room rate was £52 and the rack rate £60, the average unit efficiency rate would be 86.7 per cent. This is then multiplied by the occupancy rate to calculate the asset revenue generating efficiency index to determine what percentage of its full potential an organization is achieving. If the occupancy rate were 60 per cent, using the figures in the example just given, the asset revenue generating efficiency index would be:

86.7 per cent (average unit price efficiency rate) ×

60 per cent (occupancy rate) = 52 per cent.

It is also essential to monitor lost business opportunities by investigating why reservations offers and requests are rejected and determining whether it is to do with rate resistance, poor selling or blocking out of availability by low volume business at high demand periods.

Other performance indicators may include:

- labour co
  budget
- laundry c
  cover
- number o
- number o
- average sp
- food cost a
- analysis of

Unit costin

It is also usual
tion. Unit costi ... .s of an
activity or function which are managerially controllable to
determine the total cost. This is divided by the unit of measurement which will be dependent on the type of activity and the
organizational context. Typical units of measurement include:

- the number of pieces or kilos of linen processed per day,
  per week in the laundry
- m^2 of floor area for cleaning or maintenance
- per occupant, sleeper or room in an hotel housekeeping
  context
- per cover in the restaurant.

Computer-aided facilities management

It would seem that the majority of facilities management elements can now be computerized. Hotel software is available
for:

- reservations and yield management
- rooms management

224 Managing Facilities

communications (e.g. teleph
encing)
human resource mana
stock control
financial manag
point of sale
environm

Spec
whic
sy

one logging and video confer-

gement and administration

ement
management
ntal control.

lized facilities management software is now available
not only integrates computer-aided design and drafting
stems, but which includes other functions relating to space,
property, maintenance, contract, building systems and cable
management, asset tracking, purchasing and personnel.
Computerization facilitates:

- more effective monitoring and control of performance
- regular production of relevant statistics
- speedy identification of emerging trends.

Local area networks linking operations and sales outlets will
enhance efficiency and quality internally. Whereas wider area
networks enable an hotel to link up with other hotels, central
reservations and/or travel agents to maximize business
opportunities. Use of the internet for promotional purposes is
growing.

References and further reading

Grant Thornton Management Consultants (1987) *Management and Monitoring of Contracts for Domestic, Catering and Laundry Services – A Practical Guide and Handbook.* Nuffield Provincial Hospitals Trust .

Henley Distance Learning Ltd (1991) *Managing Operations.*

Lockwood, A., Baker, M. and Ghillyer, A. (eds) (1996) *Quality Management in Hospitality.* Cassell.

Lovelock, C.H. (1984) Strategies for managing demand in

capacity constrained service organisations. *Service Industries Journal*, 4 (3), November, 12–30.

MCI (1993) *The MCI Effective Manager, Module 2: Budgeting*. The National Forum for Management Education and Development.

8
Gaining competitive advantage

Aims and objectives

This chapter aims to:

- consider product and process developments which may be used to develop a competitive advantage
- investigate the techniques of yield management and its application to price management
- evaluate the potential of quality management in hotels
- consider the meaning and implications of improving productivity in the hotel context
- consider means of evaluating current provision and identifying opportunities for improvement.

The competitive advantage

In developing a competitive advantage, the following need to be considered:

- the product (What is its composition? What is its nature? Which features are critical or 'core' to the product?)
- the strategy of the organization (What is its mission? What are its objectives?).

Once these questions have been answered, it is appropriate to consider who else will be offering this type of product. How can the organization achieve not only better customer satisfaction than its competitors, but also customer commitment?

As was discussed in Chapter 2, 'the product' sold to hotel guests, comprises various elements (see Figure 2.1).

The core elements of this product are:

- the building and its interior and environment
- the guestroom and its facilities and appearance
- the reception and sales section.

The *service* function may be a core element in some hotels, but in budget, motel-type operations, where staff have largely been replaced by technologies (e.g. vending machines), the human service element is virtually absent. Similarly, secretarial facilities may be of enormous value to presenters at a conference, but not be appropriate in the product package offered to tourists.

Hotel managers are in the business of generating revenue from the space available to them and in Chapter 2, four basic competitive strategies were identified:

1 quality
2 provision of low-cost facilities and services, competing on price
3 distinctive provision, concentrating on product or service
4 differentiation, concentrating effort by market segmentation (i.e. developing a range of different products or services for particular segments).

Thus, the actual facilities and services provided depend on the particular hotel and the guests it targets. It must be the hotel's aim to identify the right services and facilities, of the right standard and price to satisfy the expectations of the customers, with such sensitivity to need that customer loyalty is developed.

To achieve the competitive advantage, three issues must be addressed:

1 identification of customers, their needs and expectations in terms of the whole product package, including price and the perception of value for money
2 quality – setting, achieving and continuously improving standards
3 productivity – how to achieve more with existing resources.

Continuous quality improvement

The potential which quality management offers in terms of achieving the competitive edge in any business is considerable and this has been particularly emphasized by the successful application in Japanese manufacturing industry. In an hotel situation, if return custom is to be encouraged, reputation developed or, indeed, hazard-free accommodation provided, the facilities manager must develop systems which will provide, consistently, the 'right' standard of product – and that standard must be continuously developing.

The product experience of any two customers will never be identical. The physical attributes of two guest rooms may be identical and the degree and type of service provided also may be the same, but because of the human elements – the customer and the staff involved, their interface and perceptions – the experience will be slightly different. This interaction can be controlled and pre-determined only to a certain extent. The customer will always be, to some degree, an unknown quantity.

In order to achieve total quality management, all aspects of the product need to be considered, including:

● the building, its design, interior, decor, furniture, fittings and furnishings
● the human resource and the intangible service element

- equipment and materials
- the front office functions
- the other accommodation facilities and services.

Techniques to achieve quality

Individual customers will have individual needs and a certain degree of flexibility will be needed in generating the product. The following techniques might be used (with respect to the tangible elements of the product) to achieve efficiency of operations.

- **Product design** This needs to be a continuous process, sensitive to the changing expectations of customers and also to changing solutions and processes available. The finished appearance of a guest room, for example, can be set to the required standard by the selection of appropriate decor, furnishings, fittings and furniture and by pre-determined maintenance routines.
- **Standardization** A consistent standard of quality can be better achieved where the product attributes materials for its maintenance and where services are standardized.
- **Systematic production planning** This ensures tasks which produce and maintain the product – from telephone answering and taking reservations to checking out a customer – are appropriate, systematic and productive.
- **Simplification of processes and products** By applying work study techniques, as described in Chapter 5, non-productive work can be eliminated, a steady work flow encouraged and expertise developed.
- **Matching the capacity of different equipment and processes** When this is done by careful work balancing and scheduling of tasks, it can ensure that sufficient time and other resources are available to achieve the standards required.
- **Monitoring and quality controls** As described in

Chapter 7, monitoring and other quality controls, whether these be effected by self, peer, supervisor or quality controller, can play an important role in achieving quality standards, particularly where these are on line and an integral part of the product development process.

● **Feedback mechanisms** Where errors or other deviations from standards are identified, there needs to be an effective system to investigate and address the causes of the problem to prevent re-occurrence.

In a service industry where there is frequent and direct contact between staff and customers, there must be a recognition of the part staff play in ensuring that customer perceptions are of a high quality product. Limiting the customer–staff interface to certain 'front of house' personnel can help product conformity where selection, training and supervision of these staff can focus on the 'customer encounter' and, in this way, control it. However, it is essential that there is a strong quality culture within the organization, where all staff operate as a reliable team, sharing the same quality objectives.

The concept of quality

'Quality' is not an absolute term. A product may be of a high standard or a low standard, yet still be a 'quality' product. It is the consumer's perception of whether or not a product or service fulfils a need which is important.

A small, sparsely furnished guest room, with shared bathroom facilities, is a quality product if it is perceived by the customer as consistently fulfilling his or her needs for clean and comfortable, value-for-money, overnight, accommodation. The room does not need to have silk fabric wallcoverings, state-of-the-art telecommunication systems and marble fittings in an ensuite bathroom with jacuzzi, to be of quality. Indeed, even such a room as this would not be a quality product if, for instance, on occasions the fittings were not clean or failed to function correctly.

The two rooms are of different standards, not qualities, and would appeal to different customers. This is the context in which the quality standard (BS EN ISO 9000) is written. The standard seeks to achieve conformity of quality. In an hotel, this would mean that guests could expect the same standards each time they visited the hotel. Factors which will affect the customers' perception of quality include the following.

- Price – What was paid last time? What do competitors charge? What is included? Is it good value?
- Function – Does the accommodation fulfil its purpose, including primary functions (e.g. fitness for purpose) and secondary functions (e.g. prestige, image and a feeling of well-being)?
- Reliability – Will all elements function correctly? Will a good experience of the services and facilities on the last visit be experienced on the next visit?

To produce a successful product, the facilities manager must understand the particular market segments being targeted. An assessment will be made of the specific requirements of these customers with respect to the facilities and these requirements will be translated into a standard. Quality then is customer focused. Achievement centres around satisfying the needs and expectations of the customer who is the final arbiter of quality.

Why quality management?

If customers are not satisfied by the provision at one hotel, they are likely to go to another. Indeed, even when a customer is satisfied, he or she may have nothing to lose by taking his or her custom elsewhere next time. To retain customers, it may be necessary to always add something extra to what is expected, or to 'delight' the customer. However, this must be an on-going process. If an extra was provided last time, it will be expected this time. Hence, there is a need not only for quality assurance and consistency, but also for continuous quality improvement.

The costs of poor quality in the accommodation industry can be measured in terms of:

- wasted work (the work is not to a satisfactory standard, a job has been completed incorrectly and both labour and material costs have been wasted)
- re-working (in the situation just described, perhaps the work has to be completed all over again); it is estimated that re-working alone can cost as much as 30 per cent of costs
- creation of additional work in other areas when a task has been done incorrectly
- re-inspecting
- lost custom
- liability claims
- complaints handling
- staff demotivation.

Quality costs

Conversely, quality management techniques have their own cost implications, such as:

- management time in product design, process development and in devising specifications for equipment and materials to be used
- training and development
- management time in devising documentation and procedures
- the monitoring process and equipment.

Quality controls (e.g. costs of monitoring work) can be expensive in themselves, but company slogans such as 'right first time' and 'zero defects' indicate the emphasis on preventative measures, rather than reactive measures (which are associated with poor quality). Quality may not come cheap in the short term, but long-term efficiency gains can be made, as waste is reduced, re-inspection costs and complaints eliminated, and product improvements achieved.

Establishing the standard

As discussed in Chapter 7, a standard of quality needs to be set and defined in line with the needs of the customers targeted. It isn't just a case of meeting physical requirements, they must function in the correct manner. Intangible or implicit elements (e.g. courtesy) must also be perceived by the customer.

Staff play a critical role in achieving standards of quality. Staffing decisions in terms of grades, skills, experience, numbers, hours of coverage, organization, and selection criteria are all relevant to quality, but the over-riding issue is the commitment of all staff to achieving the same standards of quality. It is the team building, the peer support and the motivation of individuals which will ultimately make continuous quality improvement a reality.

Quality terms

Many terms are used in relation to quality and it is worth considering their meanings and implications with respect to facilities management. As is shown in Figure 8.1, the overall objective would normally be a process of continuous improvement, whereby all members of the organization work together to identify improvement opportunities which will help to encourage customer loyalty.

Total quality management refers to the strategy of the organization. It implies that the executive management is committed to quality and through its actions and procedures and

Figure 8.1 Continuous quality improvement.

through the vision or mission of the organization, a culture of quality will be engendered within the organization. Such a culture will develop through a process of empowerment, whereby individuals take responsibility for their own quality standards and those of their team.

Quality assurance is achieved through the systems, standards and procedures developed to operate the hotel. These include recruitment, selection, training and development activities, which will provide all employees with the skills and knowledge required to consistently achieve the standards required. Strong team cultures can facilitate mutual support for staff, whereby problems are identified and procedures to eliminate the difficulty implemented. Such teams can best be developed through good communications systems (e.g. regular team meetings). The emphasis on quality improvement in an empowered organization means that ideas for improvement are just as likely, if not more likely, to come from operatives as they are to come from managers and, having identified problems and possible solutions, teams are given the discretion to implement the improvement. Standards of quality must be updated constantly in order to keep in line with changing requirements and any amendments must be communicated to staff through training and supervision or to contractors by specification updates. If a participative management style is used, such as quality circles, employees could well be involved in formulating quality standards.

At the bottom of the quality triangle in Figure 8.1 are assessment, control and inspection. These aspects have been discussed in Chapter 7, but again, in an empowered organization, such elements could be implemented by teams, peers or individual operatives in self-assessment processes.

Quality circles

In hotels, as in any service industry, the key to maintaining and improving standards is the motivation of the staff involved. The most effective equipment and agents may be provided, surfaces may be in excellent condition, staff may have been trained in the appropriate areas, but, without the necessary motivation, the required standard may not be achieved.

Quality circles aims to increase quality awareness and responsibility amongst staff and supervisors, at the same time as enhancing their jobs. In this way, motivation and quality improvements are linked. Quality is seen as the responsibility of all staff. Groups of workers are set up on a voluntary basis, and, in an on-going process, these staff are trained in problem-solving skills. They meet regularly to identify where quality improvements can be made (known in Japanese systems as a 'kaisan') and to develop means of tackling these problems. A less structured approach might be to have a simple 'staff suggestions scheme', whereby all staff are invited to submit proposals to improve quality or efficiency. Staff submitting suggestions which are subsequently implemented might be rewarded by a cash or other prize.

In hotels, it is not difficult to see how such techniques can be productive. Many staff, in the course of their work, will be aware of all sorts of difficulties, which affect the standard of their work. Some of these could not be identified by the facilities manager. Providing opportunities to deal with such problems would relieve frustrations, improve motivation and raise standards.

In service industries it is impossible to monitor all work completed and, therefore, the standard achieved may well be that set by the person completing the task. As described in Chapter 7, there are ways that a certain amount of the work can be monitored by a supervisor or other delegated person and this process can be used as one quality control measure.

Rather than producing high quality because work will be checked, the aim is to achieve a situation where staff achieve the standard because they have set it and they wish to achieve it.

Productivity

Productivity relates to increasing output. An increase in output does not mean that quality standards must be allowed to fall, or, conversely, that lower productivity must be accepted, if consistent quality improvements are to be achieved. Conversely, productivity improvements can go hand-in-hand with quality improvements.

Definition of productivity

Productivity is defined as:

$$\frac{\text{Output}}{\text{Input}}$$

'Input' relates to costs associated with producing the product (e.g. equipment, materials, labour and building costs) and 'output' relates the total produced.

Therefore, an increase in productivity can be achieved by:

- reducing costs and maintaining output
- maintaining costs and increasing output
- increasing costs and output, but increasing output by a disproportionate amount.

Productivity improvement may be set at four levels within an organization:

1 corporate level, where a change of policy is determined
2 systems level, where organizational aspects may be reviewed, structures redefined, procedures simplified and more efficient use made of resources
3 process level, where the process may be redesigned, new technology applied or new materials used
4 work place level, where individual workers achieve higher efficiency.

How can productivity be increased?

Many ways of improving productivity have been identified. Table 8.1 shows some of these as applied to facilities management.

Overall, methods of improving productivity can be divided into the following categories:

- scientific, where research activities produce new materials or processes
- technical, where the results of scientific research and knowledge are applied to some technology
- operational, where procedures are developed to make the best use of scientific knowledge and available technology.

Table 8.1 Approaches to increasing productivity in facilities management

Productivity increased by	Examples of application in facilities management
New technology	Automatic spreader/feeder in the laundry Computerized space management and planned maintenance Computerized environmental control
Work study	Front of house procedures, laundry processes, housekeeping and maintenance
Setting staffing levels	An on-going process must run, allowing staffing changes to meet new needs
Operating systems and procedures	Working in a team or individually Planned or reactive maintenance
Organizational management reviews	Numbers of management and supervisory grades proportional to staffing grades
Management information	Budgeting information, staff appraisals, monitoring details, market demand, income, profitability, trends, sickness and absence levels, occupancy levels, equipment life expectancy, stock levels
Bonus schemes	For consistent quality or high sales
Training	For all grades Job enrichment/multi-skilling (e.g. fitter/electrician) Retraining
Operations research	To forecast demand and staffing implications
Job design	To reduce wasted time moving from one section of the building to another Method improvement Environmental conditions
Sequencing of tasks	Particularly important for individual projects (e.g. conference planning)
Equipment scheduling and other resource utilization	To achieve optimum use of expensive equipment (e.g. compressors), but also, in the hotel context, to ensure optimum use of the facilities themselves through capacity and yield management

Scientific and technical processes must be viewed as long-term projects (e.g. the application of computer technology in environmental monitoring and control). The facilities manager can apply operational processes for shorter-term, quick returns.

Measuring productivity

Existing productivity must be evaluated and issues for subsequent investigation identified, before improvements can be made. In some situations, productivity can be measured in work study terms. For example, it is possible to measure the productivity of workers using the 'standard minute' as the basis for calculation, that is the standard or average time it should take to complete a task working at a steady, sustainable rate:

$$\frac{\text{output of work in Standard minutes (expected completion time)}}{\text{input of labour time or machine time in clock minutes (actual completion time).}}$$

In other situations, productivity may be relatively easy to calculate using the definition of productivity given earlier (output costs divided by input), for example looking at the profit and loss account of the company. Maintenance work may be measured in the number of maintenance requests responded to or the average period before requests are dealt with. In housekeeping, the output of work per hour may be calculated in terms of the number of rooms serviced per shift. In the front office, room sales might be a measure.

It is not always easy, however, to identify a unit of production by which the amount of work produced can be calculated.

Another measure of productivity appropriate for use in facilities management is by measured added value:

added value = £ (sales – costs)

the added value index = $\dfrac{\text{total employment cost}}{\text{added value.}}$

The difficulty here is that, dependent on the budgeting and accounting system used, staff and other costs from individual departments may not be available and evaluating individual impact, even of departments, on the value added is difficult.

Capacity management

In hotels, as has already been established, the facilities are a key resource and the hotel cannot be said to be working at high productivity if it is not making the most of this large capital asset. The objective is to encourage optimum space utilization for maximum, sustainable return. In general terms, the aim is to fill the rooms every night. In any business, greatest efficiency is achieved where the workload is maintained at a constant rate. In the services sector, demand cannot be totally controlled and in an hotel inevitably, there will be peaks and troughs in demand, during the day, the week and the year.

Various techniques may be used to stimulate demand at quiet periods, such as promotions and other yield management techniques, but it is unlikely that the hotel will achieve an absolutely steady capacity. To help to maximize the productivity of the staff working at any one time, their numbers need to be balanced with demand and the related workload. This can be achieved by:

- employment of part-time staff around peak times of demand
- scheduling low priority, infrequent or periodic work to smooth demand in otherwise quiet periods
- paying 'overtime' rate to full-time staff where just an odd hour is involved, instead of appointing another employee for a very short shift
- scheduling annual leave of personnel to coincide with lower demand periods or ensuring even level of absence through annual leave through scheduling
- outsourcing or contracting work at peak demand periods.

Thus, the capacity of the staff is controlled. For example, if staff are on leave, capacity is reduced, if staffing levels are 'normal', the workload can be increased by incorporating periodic tasks into the schedule.

Yield management

Balanced against productivity is demand. If demand can be kept at a constant, maximum level, regular work patterns can be established and demand is smoothed. Yield management is an approach to managing that demand.

The value of market segmentation – with respect to identification of customer needs and marketing – have been discussed in Chapter 2. In today's competitive climate, yield management uses market segmentation to enable the hotel to tune the price of the product or product package to the needs and expectations of the specific customer groups targeted, whilst maximizing profit potential. In this way, it addresses productivity by making the most of the resources available.

The elasticity of the market (i.e. the amount customers are prepared to pay for rooms) varies not only with customer expectations and perceptions of worth, but also with the economy, the feeling of well-being, the time of the year and even the weather. If hotels are to maximize their profits, the pricing of rooms must be handled sensitively.

Price flexibility

Most hotels, as well as having a standard rack rate for rooms, will vary prices (giving discount for quantity) to boost sales during low season. In business hotels, weekend breaks might be used as a means of stimulating business on off-peak days.

Two main strategies exist with respect to yield management:

- when demand is high, the emphasis is on receiving the highest rate possible for a room
- when demand is low, the emphasis is on maximizing sales through discounting.

Nevertheless, it must be realized that some market segments react with greater sensitivity to price than others. The business which has booked a sales representative in at an hotel for a specific meeting in the locality may not be swayed in its decision by the knowledge that next week the price will be cheaper. In another situation, it could be argued that to sell half the rooms in an hotel but all at full price, would be better than selling more rooms at a much reduced rate. Cleaning and heating costs would be reduced.

Yield management is a structured approach to this variable pricing practice which reflects the perishable nature of the product (a room not sold tonight, is a sale lost for ever). By practising a yield management technique, the decision as to whether or not to let an unsold room go at 6 pm for a discounted price or to hold out for a possible sale at the full price, will not simply be left to a receptionist on duty at the time.

Price reductions

Yield management can help to determine how many rooms to allocate daily for sale at various rates, for example, how many to aim to sell at full price, how many at 20 per cent reduction, how many at 50 per cent reduction and so on. These planned allocations can relate not just to periods of the year, but to specific days when fluctuations in demand are expected, one day to another and are based on:

- detailed market segmentation and analysis of the customer's spending power, expectations and product preference
- historic sales performance of each segment (e.g. pattern of demand, knowledge of local as well as national events

which attract business, knowledge of percentage of no-shows)
- current knowledge of supply and demand locally
- forecasts for the future.

Demand is forecast on a daily basis and maximum room rates are used for periods of high demand. Marketing techniques, such as promotions, are targeted on low demand periods. In calculating yield, both the average room rate and number of rooms sold are taken into account:

$$\text{yield} = \frac{\text{revenue realized}}{\text{potential revenue}} = \frac{\text{actual rooms sold} \times \text{average actual room rate}}{\text{rack rate} \times \text{rooms available}}.$$

Market analysis

Detailed market analysis is conducted into each small market segment, such as:

- demand (historic variations identified dependent on time of year, day of week, local events and frequency of need to decline business)
- lead times and reliability of bookings by different segments (probability of 'no shows')
- duration of stay
- price elasticity and perceived value of the product by guests
- average spend on other facilities and services, product packaging preferences (e.g. bed and breakfast rates or each charged separately), expectations and take-up of other facilities
- frequency of visits.

By such an analysis, an appropriate room rate is set for each segment. The objective is to target the best mix of guest types which will achieve the most profitable balance between room sales and room prices. This can only be achieved in the knowledge of yield per market segment. Despite the amount of quantitative data available and the valuable role computers and specific software packages can play in yield management, management experience and qualitative knowledge must also be used in this planning process. The overall perceived value of a particular client cannot necessarily be calculated in purely short-term financial measures. Yield management is not an exact science.

Over-booking

Cancellations and no-shows are a common phenomena of hotel room sales and must be anticipated. Some hotels have pursued a determined policy of charging guests for bookings which are not taken up, but this is not always cost effective or successful. In practising yield management, a pragmatic approach must be taken of the likelihood of some bookings not being taken up. To compensate for this, over-booking will be planned against each market segment.

Staff training in yield management

Through this process of market analysis, room prices can be set for specific market segments. Subject to demand, prices can be balanced against competition and could well vary from day to day. With this in mind, sales staff need to be well aware of the price fluctuations and trained to deal with associated guest queries. At the same time, with the detailed knowledge of the value of each sale to the hotel, incentive pay schemes related to sales can be similarly flexible.

Overall then, yield management aims to help hoteliers achieve their ultimate objective of producing the best possible return, or yield, from the space available.

Staff motivation and productivity

Well-motivated staff are of critical importance with respect to productivity within a labour-intensive industry such as that of hotels. Conditions of work, the working environment, security and job satisfaction are all important. With a well-motivated workforce many other deficiencies in the system can be overcome and productivity can be very favourably affected.

Labour turnover, absenteeism and lateness

Labour turnover, absenteeism and lateness all affect productivity. Labour turnover increases labour costs, as the costs of recruitment, selection, administration, induction and training will increase. Labour turnover is usually measured on an annual basis:

$$\text{turnover} = \frac{\text{number of leavers per annum} \times 100}{\text{average number of employees per annum}}.$$

Productivity is affected by lateness and absence as, usually, other staff have to cover key aspects of the missing operative's work and re-scheduling must occur. In the calculation of labour hours, a percentage to cover absences, sickness and lateness, as well as annual leave of staff, may be included. Although annual leave can be accurately forecast, sickness, absence and lateness cannot. In some organizations any lateness or unscheduled absence will be investigated and rigorously controlled, but it is important that any allowances made to cover such situations are realistic as over-staffing will obviously reduce productivity.

Experience/learning curve

When someone starts a new job, he or she will usually have a lot to learn in a short time. The new member of staff may be well skilled in the specific tasks to be completed, but the context of the job (including its physical location and the other people involved) must all be learned. 'The learning curve' describes this process (see figure 8.2). Much is learned initially, less in the medium term and, in the long term, very little more is learned.

During this learning process, the cost (in terms of time and materials) to complete a task drops in a regularly definable way, as the total quantity made by an individual increases. Figure 8.3 shows that, as people become competent in their job and so have less to learn, the costs reduce.

As the learner becomes more competent, he or she will complete tasks more quickly, with less waste in terms of any materials or other resources used, and require less supervisory time (i.e. less cost). As the learner becomes more and more competent, so savings become more difficult to make. Times taken to complete tasks become more difficult to reduce further and similarly any wasted work. The curve on the graph flattens out. So, in facilities management, it can be seen that, where initial staff selection is good, there are productivity advantages for maintaining a low labour turnover. Not only does high labour turnover incur replacement costs and retraining costs, but it takes time for new employees to achieve high productivity.

The experience curve has to be managed. It happens as a result of improvements in:

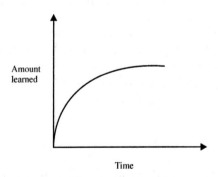

Figure 8.2 Learning–time curve.

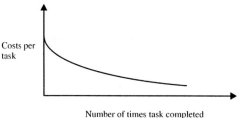

Number of times task completed

Figure 8.3 Learning–costs curve.

- staff efficiency
- staff training and development
- staff motivation
- workforce stability
- workforce organization.

Equipment and agents

The selection of appropriate equipment and agents can affect productivity by improving the speed and efficiency with which operations are completed and some of the aspects to be considered are discussed in Chapter 5. Inappropriate materials may mean that work has to be re-done, so increasing labour costs. Attention should be paid to equipment scheduling. The correct use of equipment and materials should be included in the training and development programme. This will prevent over-loading, over-use, damage to surface, equipment or staff and it will reduce effort. Personnel should be trained to maintain equipment after use, e.g. cleaning and reporting any faults.

The physical working environment

An employee who is physically and mentally comfortable in the work environment will be more productive and maintain his or her pace for longer periods. Ergonomic studies show that temperature, acoustics, humidity, lighting and other factors will affect comfort. Uniforms, dimensions of equipment used and design of the working space will also affect comfort. Therefore, the physical environment should meet the needs of staff as well as customers, if productivity is to be high. In addition, the culture of the organization needs to provide job satisfaction and a feeling of pride in the work, if staff are to be motivated and empowered to develop efficiencies.

Efficiency

Productivity relates to technical efficiency, as stated earlier. It measures output from a given input level.

It must be stressed that this is not the same as 'economic efficiency', where inputs and outputs are all priced. A department could demonstrate 'technical efficiency' by, for example, servicing more rooms to the required standard, without increasing staffing costs. This would indeed represent increased productivity. However, if these rooms were not required for letting (perhaps they had been scheduled for redecorating) it would not represent economic efficiency. There is no virtue in making goods efficiently if they are not sold! Similarly, by reducing rack rates, 100 per cent room occupancy might be achieved but increased productivity may not be the outcome.

Where servicing costs are greater than income, economic efficiency has not been achieved, hence the value of yield management measures.

Benchmarking

Benchmarking is a useful technique, whereby an hotel can compare itself either with another hotel or with some other organization. It may compare some specific aspect of its work and, where it is not leading the field, learn from others. Most hotels will evaluate last year's figures and compare them with this year's and probably look for trends over a longer period. However, by looking outside, the hotel performance can be compared and in addition scope for learning from another's experiences can be utilized.

It is relatively easy for similar hotels within a chain to compare occupancy levels or even yield percentage. Where one hotel is out-performing others, it may be worth finding out if there is some technique that is being used which can be replicated in the other hotels.

However, benchmarking does not have to be a comparison of like with like for lessons to be learned. A hotel aiming to measure the efficiency of its quality systems may learn much from a manufacturing company of some type. If there is mutual benefit (e.g. the manufacturing company may be interested in the customer handling techniques of the hotel), an agreement might be drawn up which gives each party access to information which might otherwise be restricted. In this way, organizations not in competition can learn from each other.

Product development

In achieving a competitive edge, hotels must constantly emphasize product development in an attempt to be ahead of the competition and not following it. Opportunities may be identified by staff, by customers or by management.

It is not always easy to be self-critical, but the use of objective checklists may help the manager to first analyse and evaluate current provision before developments can be identified. Post-occupancy surveys have been applied in some organizations to measure the satisfaction levels of building users and the general suitability of the work environment in new buildings. Such surveys generally consider the facility and its operation in its entirety, including the stability of its staff and the ability of the organization to attract others, its ethos and image (e.g. with respect to status and power), its functioning and the interaction of people which it either encourages or restricts.

Worthington (1995) suggests the following appraisal to evaluate buildings in terms of their (lifetime) performance:

- physical condition
- functional suitability
- space utilization
- health and safety and statutory compliance
- energy usage.

Table 8.2 shows an interior appraisal checklist. This focuses specifically on the internal, physical aspects of the hotel. It would be useful if different groups could be encouraged to complete such a questionnaire to provide different perceptions of the physical components of the hotel's product.

In answering these questions, weaknesses in the product may be identified, whether these be weaknesses in terms of meeting customer expectations, quality standards or efficiency standards. Strategies to address these can then be identified and priorities determined. The example shown addresses only part of one core feature of the product – the building and its interior/environment. (Other core features defined were the guest room and its facilities and appearance and the reception and sales section.) Similar checklists could be produced for the building exterior, the guest room and reception/sales function, or indeed for any of the non-core features.

Product development must be on-going. An approach to this process of continual review is shown in Figure 8.4.

Reviewing the facilities

A review might be appropriate:

- at the end of the financial year
- at the end of a busy season

Table 8.2 Interior appraisal checklist

Function
Define briefly what you think is the function of the interior

Space
Is the organization of the space efficient in coping practically with the activities accommodated?
How would you describe the spatial quality (e.g. open, closed, indifferent, complex, etc.)?
Is the spatial quality appropriate to the function?
Are the views outside and into adjacent spaces important?
If 'yes', does the furniture layout take this into account?

Light
Is the lighting level and distribution efficient for the activities?
How does the lighting affect the form of the interior? Does it flatten the form or make it more articulate and three-dimensional?
Is there a logical relationship between the lighting plan and the furniture and IT?
What type of artificial light is used?
What effect does the artificial light have on the colours and textures of the interior finishes and materials?
What role does lighting play, or fail to play, in generating the right atmosphere?
How easy is the lighting to clean and re-lamp? Is control adequate?
How energy efficient is the lighting system?

Colour
Is the colour scheme practical for durability and appearance?
What part does colour play, or not play, in the generation of atmosphere?
How are colours affected by lighting (natural and artificial)?

Materials/texture
Are the materials practical for durability and maintenance?
How do the materials affect the atmosphere?
Are textural qualities amplified or flattened by the lighting system?
Is there an interesting variety of textures or is there a lack of contrast?

---

continued

Table 8.2 Continued

What effect do the materials have on the acoustic environment?
Is the use of pattern satisfactory?

Furniture
Is the layout of the furniture practical for use, movement and circulation?
Is the furniture practical and comfortable, anthropometrically correct and easy to move (if it is intended to be moved often)?
How does the furniture relate to the lighting plan?
Does the furniture integrate visually with the context of the room?
Where required, does the furniture layout assist social interaction among users?

Acoustics
What are the main sources of noise in the room? Is the noise suitably controlled?
How do the materials in the space increase or reduce the noise level?

Heating and ventilation
Are the heating and ventilation systems appropriate in terms of comfort?
Are the visual appearance of the heating and ventilation appliances satisfactory?
Are controls adequate and sensibly located?
How energy efficient are the heating and ventilation systems?

IT
Is operation clear, with controls and instructions sensibly located?
Is the appearance of the units in harmony with the overall room appearance?
Are the units comfortable to use?
Are heat and sound emissions suitably managed?
How does the IT relate to the lighting plan?
Where necessary, does the IT layout encourage social interaction (e.g. televisions)?
Are suitable energy efficiencies applied?

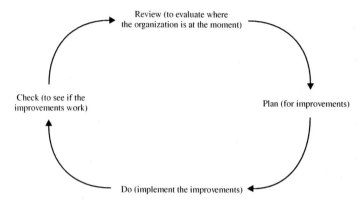

Figure 8.4 The product development review cycle.

- during a slack period
- after implementing a new procedure
- following a complaint or other incident
- when contemplating outsourcing.

The review may be focused on one activity or facility related to the product or may be designed to consider much broader ranging issues. Most reviews have more value if they are conducted by more than one person, the quality circle would be an obvious group to involve, customers would be another and there is often great benefit to be derived from an outside source. A consultant might be used for this purpose, a manager from a different hotel within the group or a supplier with whom there is a strategic alliance (and there will, therefore, be benefits for the supplier if the business develops). There are issues of confidentiality of commercially sensitive issues when outsiders are involved, but means of involving such groups can usually be found.

Issues could include:

- product components – their value, popularity and delivery
- size and capacity of operation and facilities – its suit-ability, usage, strengths and weaknesses

- the operating climate – the opportunities and threats, sales forecasts and trends
- quality – the implementation of continuous improvement
- health, safety and security of staff, customers and other building users
- the staff – their skills, turnover, availability and morale
- environmental impact, energy and waste reduction
- pricing and credit management
- effects of recent legislation
- marketing and promoting the product.

Having identified opportunities for developing the product (review), the next stage is planning the improvement followed by implementation and checking. Obviously there is no value in identifying opportunities if ideas are not taken forward. In some cases, implementation may not be feasible for some time, in other cases they may be put in place immediately.

The important issue is that the product is not allowed to stagnate, even if, at the moment it is doing well. If the hotel business is to grow, then in a culture of continuous improvement, all staff should be involved in an on-going process of planning and product development.

References and further reading

Armistead, C., Johnston, R. and Slack, N. (1988) The strategic determinants of service productivity. In (R. Johnston, ed.) *Management of Service Operations*.

Becker, F.D. (1990) *The Total Workplace: Facilities Management and The Elastic Organisation*. Praeger.

Becker, F.J. (1989) They drink beer, don't they? *Facilities Design and Management*, 18(5).

Kunst, P. and Lemmink, J. (1996) *Managing Service Quality*. Paul Chapman.

Lockwood, A., Gummesson, E., Hubrecht J. and Senior, M. (1993) Developing and maintaining a strategy for service quality. In R. Teare and M. Olsen (eds) *International Hospitality Management*. Pitman.

Worthington, D. (1995) Strategic Property Management. In (A. Spedding ed.) *Facilities Management Handbook*.

Index